WHAT WORKS

How Local Governments Have Made the Leap from Measurement to Management

WHAT WORKS

How Local Governments Have Made the Leap from Measurement to Management

ICMA RESULTS NETWORKS
Center for Performance Measurement™

ICMA advances professional local government worldwide. Its mission is to create excellence in local governance by developing and advancing professional management of local government. ICMA, the International City/County Management Association, provides member support; publications, data, and information; peer and results-oriented assistance; and training and professional development to more than 9,000 city, town, and county experts and other individuals and organizations throughout the world. The management decisions made by ICMA's members affect 185 million individuals living in thousands of communities, from small villages and towns to large metropolitan areas.

The ICMA Center for Performance Measurement™ (CPM) is dedicated to helping local governments improve the effectiveness and efficiency of public services through the collection, analysis, and application of performance information. To learn more about CPM, please visit icma.org/performance or call 202/962-3562.

To order additional copies of this book or other ICMA publications, please visit icma.org/press or call 800/745-8780.

Library of Congress Cataloging-in-Publication Data

What works : how local governments have made the leap from measurement to management / ICMA Center for Performance Measurement. -- 3rd ed.
p. cm.
ISBN 978-0-87326-181-4
1. Local government--United States. 2. Total quality management in government--United States. 3. Municipal services--United States. 4. County services--United States. I. International City/County Management Association. Center for Performance Measurement.
JS331.H68 2008
352.140973--dc22

2008037284

©2008 by the International City/County Management Association, 777 North Capitol Street, NE, Suite 500, Washington, DC 20002. All rights reserved, including rights of reproduction and use in any form or by any means, including the making of copies by any photographic process, or by any electrical or mechanical device, printed, written, or oral or recording for sound or visual reproduction, or for use in any knowledge or retrieval system or device, unless permission in writing is obtained from the copyright proprietor.

Design: Charles E. Mountain
Robert D. Mench

Printed in the United States of America

2013 2012 2011 2010 2009 2008 2007

5 4 3 2

Contents

Preface vii
Acknowledgments ix
Introduction xi
High Performance Management Practices 1
Code Enforcement 27
Facilities Management 35
Fire and EMS 49
Fleet Management 65
Highways & Road Maintenance 73
Housing 79
Human Resources 87
Information Technology 93
Library Services 101
Parks and Recreation 115
Police Services 123
Purchasing 141
Refuse and Recycling 147
Risk Management 161
Youth Services 169
ICMA Center for Performance Measurement™ Information/Enrollment Form 177

Preface

In good times or challenging ones, an effective system of performance measurement is an essential management tool for any organization. In this book, the ICMA Center for Performance Measurement™ (CPM) presents more than 70 real-world examples of how local governments are using performance measurement to

- Boost service-delivery performance
- Monitor progress toward objectives
- Manage scarce resources well.

It is our hope that these examples will inspire and motivate similar efforts in other organizations.

Inside you'll see

- How the city of Charlottesville, Virginia, used comparative performance information from CPM to determine that it was paying more for electricity than many of its in-state neighbors, and how Charlottesville then tested a load-shedding technique that saved more than $16,000 when it was implemented in just one elementary school this past year. Based on the success of that pilot test, the city is projected to save $350,000 this fiscal year when the technique is implemented citywide.
- How the city of Casper, Wyoming, used CPM data to discover its higher-than-average police vehicle accident rate—and then it reduced that rate by 10 percent.
- How the city of Dallas, Texas, evaluated and reduced its code enforcement cycle time by more than half using performance measurement.
- And, much more!

I hope you find *What Works* useful. To share your performance measurement success story—and possibly be featured in a future edition of *What Works*—please send a message to cpmmail@icma.org.

Robert J. O'Neill Jr.
Executive Director
International City/County Management Association

Acknowledgments

This book was made possible through the contributions and support of many individuals. The first to be thanked are the managers, administrators, primary coordinators, and service-area specialists who so generously shared their time and knowledge as they discussed how they apply performance measurement in their jurisdictions. Their dedication to improving the delivery of local government services—and, by extension, the quality of life in their communities—is apparent in the information that they share in this book. Their work represents a source of inspiration for all who work in public service.

*****

Mary Marik copyedited this book. Valerie Hepler and Charles Mountain created the design for the book and attended to the many particulars necessary to publish it. Ann Mahoney provided tremendous production support as well. Allison King and Ellen Foreman offered excellent marketing advice.

For the ICMA Center for Performance Measurement™, Louise Snyder led in the planning, research, and writing for this book, with considerable support from Kira Hasbargen. Donald Gloo, Tom Holland, Nish Keshav, Philip Mancini, Mark Thompson, and Gerald Young participated in the research and writing as well. The thorough and thoughtful research of all constitutes the backbone of this book. To all: Thank you for your long hours and dedication to the success of this specific project as well as your steadfast belief in the importance and vitality of local governments and the citizens they serve.

Michael Lawson
Director, ICMA Center for Performance Measurement™

Introduction

What Works?—Performance Measurement Works!

ICMA's executive director, Bob O'Neill, posits that there is a performance dividend enjoyed by communities that employ a professional manager. The ICMA Center for Performance Measurement™ (CPM) extends this notion by suggesting that there is also a performance dividend to be derived by communities that engage in performance measurement—and the stories presented in *What Works* are intended to help demonstrate this performance dividend of performance measurement.

CPM seeks to assist local governments with the collection, analysis, and application of performance information in pursuit of the ultimate outcomes of

- Improving local government service delivery
- Informing local government management and policy decisions
- Helping local governments manage resources as effectively as possible in an increasingly resource-constrained environment.

The stories presented in What Works *are intended to help demonstrate the performance dividend of performance measurement.*

CPM has been pursuing this mission since 1994, when it first began working with a core group of approximately 40 large cities and counties in the United States that were interested in adding a peer comparison component to their existing performance measurement systems. Those early years were devoted to the

- Selection and definition of comparable performance measures
- Development of effective data collection instruments
- Establishment of rigorous data cleaning methods
- Creation of informative data reports.

But long before CPM was created, ICMA had been engaged in performance measurement. ICMA published articles in the late 1930s in its *Public Management* magazine on performance measurement (for example, measuring code enforcement, fire services, and a host of other local government services). These articles, in turn, were compiled and published by ICMA in 1943 in a book aptly titled, *Measuring Municipal Services.* It was coauthored by ICMA Executive Director Clarence Ridley and ICMA staff member Herbert Simon—who was a graduate student at the University of Chicago at the time and who, much later in his career, would go on to win a Nobel Prize in economics.

CPM's participant base now includes more than 220 cities, towns, counties, boroughs, villages, special districts, and other local government agencies across North America. (A number of military bases, which function much like local governments, have also participated over the years.) CPM's operations have also grown: from the simple collection, cleaning, and reporting of performance information of earlier years to today's:

- **Regional consortium support and expansion—**As a complement to the full-service North American program, CPM also offers opportunities for regional analysis and support through a number of regional consortia. A list of CPM's regional consortia is available at http://icma.org/performance.
- **Special-interest consortium development—**CPM is also building a network of special-interest consortia, which provide to communities analysis and interaction opportunities based on common characteristics like size or local industry. CPM recently established the Small Communities Consortium to serve the interests of communities with populations 20,000 and smaller, and plans are in the works for a university-town consortium and other special-interest consortia.
- **More user-friendly reporting—**CPM has published a data-based annual report since the program's inception in 1994. Since then, the report has evolved from an attempt to share all data to a more focused exposition of participants' performance on "core measures." In 2008, CPM introduced a suite of reports—including the long-standing *Annual Data Report* and a new dashboard report that provides a snapshot of each participant's performance on a number of CPM's core measures. The goal is to provide performance information in a number of formats, each tailored to a different audience.

This new edition of *What Works* represents yet another step in CPM's evolution.

In 2007, CPM committed itself to gathering stories from more than half of the veteran participants each year, stories that demonstrate the performance dividends those participants have gained from engaging in performance measurement—both through CPM and other avenues. (Veteran participants include those who have participated in CPM for two or more data cycles.) This book shares a large complement of those stories.

Stories were developed in a number of ways:

- Mining CPM data to find high-performing jurisdictions on many of CPM's core measures and asking them how they achieved their exceptional performance levels
- Following up on media reports of high performance; for example, asking staff in Colorado Springs, Colorado, which local government programs may have led to the city's selection as one of *Money* magazine's top places to live in 2006
- Soliciting participants directly for stories of how they
  - Use performance information to inform day-to-day management and policy decisions
  - Share performance information with elected officials, the public, and other audiences

  - Link performance measures to organizationwide goals expressed in their strategic plans and other documents
  - Promote individual accountability for organizational performance.

The continuous-learning model versus the "gotcha" model of performance measurement

It is important to note, too, that another intention of this book is to emphasize CPM's focus on the continuous-learning model of performance measurement. This model promotes performance measurement as tool for

- Evaluating performance
- Setting improvement targets
- Finding proven methods for doing better.

The continuous-learning model specifically eschews the idea of using performance measurement to root out malingerers or punish poor performance, which some have dubbed the "gotcha" model of performance measurement.

Performance measurement will never be embraced by employees or enculturated by the organization if it is used as a stick rather than a carrot. Moreover, the organization will not realize the full potential—the learning potential—of performance measurement if employees are punished rather than rewarded for identifying targets for improvement.

A great example of how one jurisdiction—Fishers, Indiana—is capitalizing on the learning potential of performance measurement appears in Chapter 1. Fishers is using its performance measurement program to examine snow removal performance and find ways to improve—using citizen opinion as the driver. Take a look!

Performance measurement encourages movement from good to great

As Jim Collins identifies in his book, *Good to Great: Why Some Companies Make the Leap—and Others Don't,* organizations that have moved from good to great share three qualities:

- Piercing clarity of mission
- Rigorous assembling of evidence
- Rigorous application of logic and questioning.[1]

CPM recommends local governments use performance measurement to prompt and answer several key questions[2] that encourage development of these qualities:

- To develop piercing clarity of mission, local governments must ask:
  - Are we doing the right "what"—and according to whom?
  - Who is "we"?
  - Why pursue high performance—and what is at stake if we do?
- To promote rigorous assembling of evidence, ask:
  - How do residents view our performance?

- — Are we good at what we do—and if so, how good are we?
- — What is the appropriate level of performance for us?
- — How do we know if we are reaching our appropriate performance level?

- To promote rigorous application of logic and questioning, ask:
  - — How do we improve—and what real or assumed constraints get in the way?
  - — What can we learn from high performers?—with "high" being defined broadly to include not only the best overall but also the best at leveraging resources, the most improved, and perhaps others.
  - — How do we avoid mindless mimicry?

What Works includes a number of examples of communities that are using performance measurement to ask just these questions. See Chapter 1 for specifics.

How to use *What Works* in your own move from good to great

Readers of *What Works* can use the featured case studies to begin—or accelerate—their organization's move from good to great:

If you just have a few minutes:

- Select a mini case study from a relevant chapter and present it as food for thought at a management team, individual department, or other staff meeting. Use it to ask this question: What can we learn and apply from high performers?
- Make a short presentation to staff about the importance of measuring performance, with an eye toward making more informed decisions or improving service rather than for the sake of measuring. Use it to emphasize the importance of "rigorously assembling evidence."

If you have an hour or so:

- Pick one or two case studies of particular interest. Arrange a time to talk with the contact person(s) listed to learn more. This helps answer the question: What can we learn and apply from high-performing local governments?
- Select a mini case study and use it to launch a brainstorming session about how well your own organization's performance in this area supports the organization's mission—and how you might adjust performance if stronger connection to the mission is required. Assign specific employees to follow up on the suggestions generated. This supports establishment of "piercing of clarity of mission."

If you have a few hours—or even a whole day:

- Use one of the case studies to launch a discussion with staff, elected officials, or citizens about how to
  - — Use performance information to inform decisions

— Link performance measures to department or organization goals

— Select appropriate targets for improving service.

This supports all three good-to-great practices.

- Investigate one of the reporting methods shared by a jurisdiction in Chapter 1. One interesting example is Cartersville, Georgia's method of sharing citizen survey results at city council meetings. Consider how you might implement a similar reporting style in your jurisdiction. This supports both "rigorous assembling of evidence" and "rigorous application of logic."
- Ask a staff member to research an effective management practice already in use in your jurisdiction. Ask that person to determine performance levels relevant to the practice, interview appropriate staff, and write a short summary similar to the case studies in this book. Share the case study with appropriate staff—and CPM! (Just e-mail it to cpmmail@icma.org, and we can share it in an upcoming edition of *What Works,* or another outlet.) Encourage staff to use this case study approach when evaluating other practices. Like the previous suggestion, this supports both "rigorous assembling of evidence" and "rigorous application of logic."
- Choose a performance indicator that is particularly important to your jurisdiction. Use CPM's annual data report to find the top performers on that indicator. Contact a few of the top performers to find out which practices they are using to achieve their high-performance levels. Evaluate the practices to determine whether they might work in your jurisdiction. (A recommended procedure is provided in the next section.) This supports the "rigorous assembling of evidence" and "rigorous questioning."

How can I be sure that what works in one community will work in mine?

In short, there is no guarantee that any practice used in one community will work in another. However, the practices presented in *What Works* are proven practices, and whether they are adopted by your jurisdiction without change or adapted to your jurisdiction's unique circumstances, they represent options for promoting movement from good to great—or whatever outcome you may be seeking—by

- Streamlining your performance measurement program
- Refining your decision-making processes
- Boosting performance, either organizationwide or within a specific service area.

Remember that some element of risk taking is always required when attempting improvement or making other tough management decisions. By considering your options carefully and making an educated choice as to which one is best, you increase the likelihood of success.

If you think you are ready for a change, consider the following guidelines for ensuring the best possible outcome from your efforts:

1. **Measure your current performance level.**
2. **Assess priorities—that is, consider carefully whether a change is warranted.** Although it may sound obvious, first make sure that a change in performance level is desired. Because most local governments operate in a limited-resource environment, it is important to direct resources toward boosting performance in areas of greatest need.

   Being the best—or nearly the best—in every service area is not necessarily an appropriate goal. Because your resources are probably limited, be sure to assess priorities (through citizen surveys, consultation with elected officials, and other means) and direct resources toward providing the highest level of service in your priority areas.

   Because most local governments operate in a limited-resource environment, it is important to direct resources toward boosting performance in areas of greatest need.

   One tool available to help local governments determine citizen priorities is the key driver analysis (KDA) now offered as a component of the National Citizen Survey™. KDA is a private sector, market research tool recently incorporated into the National Citizen Survey™ to identify the small set of key services that have the most impact in shaping citizens' overall satisfaction with their particular local government. (More information about the National Citizen Survey™ is available at http://icma.org/ncs.)

   If you determine after this assessment process that a change is needed, proceed to the next step.

3. **Find out who is doing it better—and how they are doing it.** Don't reinvent the wheel. See what others are doing, and determine whether wholesale adoption or adaptation of one of their practices is more appropriate.

   In your search, consider jurisdictions that are different from yours as well as those that are alike. Keep in mind that you may find good ideas next door or across the continent, in a jurisdiction just like yours or in a jurisdiction entirely different.

   To help in your decision about which jurisdictions might be appropriate for comparison, CPM provides the following information about jurisdictions featured in this book and in its other reports:

   — **Jurisdiction profiles**—Abbreviated profiles accompany each case study, showing each jurisdiction's population, number of square miles, median household income, and form of government. More detailed profile information is available in each of CPM's annual data reports—and to participants via CPM's private Web site (http://icma.org/cpm). (Just click on the year of the data you would like to view, and then select the service area. If you want general information not tied to a service area, click on the link to the general demographic data.)

— **Service-delivery characteristics**—Within individual service areas, consider how jurisdictions provide service. Most case studies include this sort of detail. It is also available in the printed data report and in the data sets available through CPM's participants-only private Web site (http://icma.org/cpm).

4. **Pick the best of the best, and adopt or adapt the practice.** In some cases you might be able to adopt another jurisdiction's practice exactly as it is being used, but you might also need to adapt it in order for it to work in your jurisdiction. Also consider the particular kind of "best" of most importance to your community. Try looking beyond only those that are "top in class" for best practices. For communities with modest resources, best might be defined as communities that produce above-average results with below-average resources. For those jurisdictions with well-below-average results, the kind of best of most interest might be those jurisdictions that made significant improvements in a relatively short span of time.
5. **Measure your service level again.** After the new practice has been in effect for a period of time—perhaps several months or a year (or in some cases more time)—you will want to figure out whether it has had the desired effect.
   — **If the service level meets the priorities** set by your organization (whether by citizens, elected officials, or departments), continue with your new practice, and continue measuring to ensure that your service level remains where you want it to be.
   — **If the service level does not meet the priorities** set by your organization (whether by citizens, elected officials, or departments), determine whether it is best to continue with this new practice, return to your previous practice, or try another practice. When making your decision, consider the size of the gap between your current performance level and your ultimate goal. If the distance is relatively small, perhaps it would be best to continue with your new practice for a little longer. Also, be sure to consider the impact that your decision will have on citizen satisfaction and staff morale—of course, you will want to optimize both.

Other performance measurement resources

CPM—and ICMA more broadly—offer a wide range of resources designed to help local governments achieve their performance measurement goals. Many are available to anyone, but some are available only to CPM participants.

ICMA's performance measurement resources available to anyone:

- **CPM's public Web site**—Available at http://icma.org/performance, this site is packed with information about CPM services and performance measurement in general.
- **CPM certificate program**—CPM offers this annual recognition opportunity to all local government entities that apply and demonstrate an

exceptional commitment to the application of performance measurement to improve service delivery. Applications may be downloaded at http://icma.org/performance.

- **ICMA consulting services**—Interested in augmenting your jurisdiction's performance measurement capabilities? Try ICMA Consulting Services. Some of our focus areas are performance measurement and management systems, strategic planning and visioning, and process improvement, among others. Ask for a free mini consultation or a description of our on-site assessments. E-mail consultingservices@icma.org or call 202/962-3585 for more information.
- **ICMA University workshops and audioconferences**—Please visit http://icma.org/ and click on "ICMA University" at the top of the page for an up-to-date listing of all offerings.
- ***Performance Matters* e-newsletter**—You can have this information-packed, monthly newsletter sent to your e-mail account by placing a request at http://icma.org/performancematters.
- **Performance Management Track at the ICMA Annual Conference**—Open to all ICMA Conference attendees, this track features conference sessions, workshops, and other events designed to maximize your organization's benefit from engaging in performance measurement. Information about this track and the conference itself is available at http://icma.org/conference.

Resources only for CPM participants include:

- **CPM's private Web site**—The site can be accessed at http://icma.org/cpm. If your local government is a paid CPM participant, and you need a password, just click on the "Password Lookup & Changes" link in the bottom left-hand corner of the page. From there, you can set up a new password—or request a reminder your existing password. Resources available on the site include:
  - — Electronic data submission system
  - — Electronic copies of the annual data report—to download and share with staff anytime
  - — All CPM data beginning with FY 1996
  - — A query and graphing tool for extracting and analyzing CPM data
  - — Electronic forums for exchanging ideas and topics of interest with participants
  - — Contact information to promote networking with fellow participants
  - — Much more.
- **Rigorous data collection, cleaning, and reporting**—CPM provides participants with annual performance data collection and processing services—including rigorous cleaning and verification of all information submitted to ensure strong data reliability. Data are collected in 15 different service areas—and can be submitted for one of two deadlines,

depending on when your jurisdiction's fiscal year ends. The list of service areas is available at http://icma.org/performance.

- **Regional and special-interest consortia**—All participants are eligible to participate in CPM's regional and special-interest consortia at no additional cost. These consortia enhance the regular program by facilitating comparisons and other networking activities among communities sharing regional or other interests. Consortia participants also benefit from consortium-specific reporting and meeting opportunities.

To learn more about CPM—including how to join—please visit http://icma.org/performance or e-mail cpmmail@icma.org. (An inquiry form is also included at the back of this book.)

Notes

1. Similar concepts also are found in Jeffrey Pfeffer and Robert Sutton, "Evidence-Based Management," *Harvard Business Review* (January 2006): 63–74.
2. Source of most of the following questions: Commonwealth Centers for High Performance Organizations, Inc., Charlottesville, Va., www.highperformanceorg.com.

High Performance Management Practices

High Performance Management Practices

City of Cartersville, GA

Reporting citizen survey results

For the city of Cartersville, conducting a biennial citywide survey is an essential way to gauge citizens' satisfaction with what they are getting for their tax dollars.

The city of Cartersville has a long history of conducting citizen surveys. Prior to enrolling with the National Citizen Survey™ (NCS) in 2003, the city used other survey services to gain citizen feedback. Although results from previous surveys were helpful, the results did not permit the level of analysis that the city desired. Wanting to ask citizens customized questions and develop reliable trend data, the city of Cartersville began to research other survey instruments. The city ultimately chose NCS because of its customization options, ability to track trends, and affiliation with ICMA.

City council meetings have emerged as the ideal outlet for survey results... because the meetings are broadcast on radio and television and reach a wide audience.

Other NCS features that appealed to Cartersville included

- Customized survey form
- Customized cover letter accompanying survey form
- Three mailings each to 1,200 randomly selected households
- Data coding and cleaning
- Comparisons of results with weighted population norms
- Executive summary and statistical analysis of survey results
- Access to technical assistance.

The NCS also offers at additional cost larger mailings, Spanish-language surveys, open-ended questions, Web-based surveys, and presentation of results to elected officials (and others).

It's all about your audience

After receiving the survey results from the NCS, Cartersville staff began to brainstorm ways in which to report the results. Wanting to balance the competing demands of sharing the results as much as possible with keeping the report as easily digestible as possible, staff decided to report a portion of the survey results at the end of each council meeting. Survey results are also reported in the city's newsletter and published on the city's Web site.

In the report of survey results at Cartersville's city council meetings, the city manager, Sam Grove, spends approximately 10 minutes explaining the results from one section of the survey. A question-and-answer session follows.

City council meetings have emerged as the ideal outlet for survey results in Cartersville because the meetings are broadcast on radio and television

Case Profile

Population:
20,568

Square miles:
28

Median household income:
$41,162

Form of government:
Council-manager

For additional information about the practices described in this case study, please contact Elaine Edwards, assistant to city manager, at eedwards@cityofcartersville.org.

and reach a wide audience. Councilmembers themselves have said that they find the presentations very useful and informative. Moreover, councilmembers frequently refer to results from the presentations when discussing key policy issues.

Reporting in action

An example of how to use results from citizen surveys to inform local government decisions can be seen in the city of Cartersville's process for implementing transportation impact fees.

In 2003, Cartersville took advantage of the NCS option to add customized questions to its survey, and it asked residents whether they would support the introduction of transportation impact fees. Survey results showed that only 49 percent of residents either strongly supported or somewhat supported the use of transportation impact fees to fund road improvements. Based on these results, the city decided not to implement the fees at that time.

In its 2005 NCS survey, the city included the transportation impact fee question again. This time, 75 percent of respondents indicated that they either strongly supported or somewhat supported the fees. The results were reported at a city council meeting, informing the council and the public that the majority of residents supported the introduction of transportation impact fees—and the council voted to implement the fees.

Cartersville has also used the NCS to guide policy on such issues as support for a sales tax-funded civic center and the establishment of a stormwater utility. Going forward, the city plans to use customized survey questions to guide decisions on greenspace management, tree ordinances, and redevelopment districts.

City of Casper, WY

Case Profile

Population:
51,738

Square miles:
26

Median household income:
$49,519

Form of government:
Council-manager

Use performance data to develop the right questions—and improve performance

For FY 2006, the city of Casper reported 3.82 vehicle accidents per 100,000 miles driven by law enforcement vehicles. The mean and median values for all jurisdictions reporting that year were 1.52 and 1.20, respectively. Thus, the city's police vehicle accident rate was somewhat high compared with other ICMA Center for Performance Measurement™ (CPM) communities, and city staff were concerned.

Why was the police vehicle accident rate so high?

When Casper staff compared the city's FY 2006 law enforcement vehicle accident data with that reported by other CPM communities, they found that Casper performed among the lowest of all. To determine why Casper's performance was so low, staff began an exhaustive research process.

Was it the snow?

The first hypothesis they considered was that Casper's snowy winter weather was causing the high number of police vehicle accidents. After controlling for weather, however, Casper staff found that the city's performance was still not good compared with other CPM communities.

No, it was the support columns in the police garage!

Further review of Casper's police vehicle accident data revealed that 27 of the previous 35 accidents (over approximately two years) involved vehicles hitting support columns in the police department parking garage. An assessment of the garage indicated that parking spaces were narrower than normal and that the support columns were difficult to see when staff were parking vehicles, thus promoting collisions with the columns.

Might pink columns help?

To make parking easier—and possibly reduce the number of collisions—the city decided to widen the parking spaces and paint the support columns a "shocking Pepto-Bismol pink." Department leaders also emphasized the importance of maneuvering vehicles carefully in the garage to prevent further accidents.

The result of these actions was that in the year following the change, there were no incidents of police vehicles striking columns in the garage. Also, expenditures for losses related to police vehicle accidents dropped by almost half, from $63,541 in FY 2006 to $33,821 in FY 2007.

For additional information about the practices described in this case study, please contact Jesse Springer, administrative analyst, at jspringer@cityofcasperwy.com.

City of Colorado Springs, CO

Case Profile

Population:
394,914

Square miles:
194

Median household income:
$47,854

Form of government:
Council-manager

Can performance measurement and strategic planning promote livability?

In 2006, *Money* magazine put Colorado Springs first on its big-city "Best Places to Live" list—and the city government is proud of the designation. Colorado Springs has employed a professional manager since 1920 and has participated in the ICMA Center for Performance Measurement™ (CPM) since 1998. Is it possible that these factors helped Colorado Springs develop its reputation as one of America's most desirable places to live?

Former city manager Lorne Kramer suggested that the "use of performance measures in our guiding document, the Strategic Action Plan, has been invaluable in achieving our city's vision of being the community of choice for living, working, and leisure. Measuring our city's performance gives us the information to provide more effective and efficient municipal services as well as improve accountability and trust in government." While Colorado Springs's reputation as one of the best places to live is certainly not wholly attributable to its commitment to performance measurement, the commitment itself reflects the values of high-quality service, accountability, and transparency in municipal government that helped propel the city to its position on *Money*'s list.

City staff say that participating in CPM allows them to "compare performance with that of other entities of similar size or characteristics and provides the information needed to benchmark performance against those jurisdictions to determine if there are steps that can be taken to improve the efficiency or quality of the services provided." Staff further report that deliberate steps are taken to integrate the city's performance measures with its strategic plan—and the measures are used by staff and elected officials to track the city's progress toward achieving each strategic plan objective.

For more information about the practices described in this case study, please contact Charae T. Sachanandani, principal analyst, at 719/385-5856 or csachanandani@springsgov.com.

City of Coral Springs, FL

Case Profile

Population:
131,257

Square miles:
24

Median household income:
$63,197

Form of government:
Council-manager

Baldrige National Quality Award

Established in the 1980s, the Malcolm Baldrige National Quality Awards program seeks to "enhance the competitiveness, quality, and productivity of U.S. organizations for the benefit of all residents" through application of its rigorous "Criteria for Performance Excellence." The program also invites organizations using the criteria to apply for its annual Malcolm Baldrige National Quality Awards that recognize service delivery and business process excellence in several sectors. Details about the criteria and awards can be found at www.quality.nist.gov/.

Baldrige's government pilot in 2006

Previously open only to business, health care, and education organizations, in 2006 the Baldrige program initiated a pilot under which governments and nonprofit organizations were invited to apply for performance feedback but not actual awards. The city of Coral Springs elected to participate in this pilot and in its application used data collected through its participation in the ICMA Center for Performance Measurement™ (CPM) as evidence of high service delivery performance.

If the analysis reveals another jurisdiction performing better than Coral Springs on a particular indicator, city staff contact that jurisdiction and ask about the specific metric and how the high performance was achieved.

First government award in Baldrige program

In 2007, when the award competition was officially opened to government and nonprofit organizations, Coral Springs became the first state or local government to be awarded the honor.

The city's long history of commitment to quality and customer satisfaction goes back 15 years, when it first adopted the Baldrige criteria as a guide to providing best-in-class services to its residents and businesses at the lowest possible price.

Coral Springs's city manager, Michael S. Levinson, says, "I'm often asked, 'Why Baldrige?' The answer is simple: exceptional customer satisfaction ratings and performance results, and our ability to sustain these results in the best of times and the worst of times."

CPM participation bolsters city's Baldrige efforts

In addition to gathering evidence for Baldrige, Coral Springs also looks at its own trend data regularly and compares its performance with the performance of other CPM jurisdictions. If the analysis reveals another jurisdiction performing better than Coral Springs on a particular indicator, city staff

For additional information about the practices described in this case study, please contact Chelsea Stahl, performance measurement analyst, at cstahl@coralsprings.org.

contact that jurisdiction and ask about the specific metric and how the high performance was achieved. Coral Springs finds that this research provides some of the best payoff from its CPM participation.

Town of Fishers, IN

Ensure the relevance of the measures themselves

When discussing the participation of Fishers in the ICMA Center for Performance Measurement™ (CPM) and performance measurement generally, town officials note that their use of performance measurement has evolved over the years. When the town first began measuring service delivery performance in 2006, departments chose their own indicators. These initial indicators were chosen for a couple of reasons:

- Representation of the most readily available data
- Reflection of the most common outputs of the departments.

Although this represented a good first step, a shortcoming of this early set of indicators was that few related directly to council goals or departmental outcomes.

Track results over time and compared with peers

In 2007, Fishers changed the way it selects departmental performance measures. Measures are now synchronized with council, town manager, and departmental outcomes and goals. Moreover, results are compared with Fishers's own performance in prior years and with the CPM median. The town began cross comparisons in 2007 and also an intensive review of the measurements in 2007. Beginning with the 2007 budget, CPM data were incorporated into the budget. The town is building a database of its key indicators with results for each year since 2007 although it includes data since 2005.

Act on results

The town not only collects and tracks performance information; it also acts on the results. The town manager meets twice each month and several times throughout the month individually with department heads, during which the departments' performance on key indicators and strategies for capitalizing on successes and improving performance where it is warranted are often discussed. These meetings work toward promoting day-to-day management of departmental operations according to organizationwide goals.

Ensure accountability

Fishers also uses performance measurement data to justify annual budget requests and inform the personnel evaluations of department heads and executive staff.

Case Profile

Population:
62,725

Square miles:
29.4

Median household income:
$75,638

Form of government:
Council-manager

For additional information about the practices described in this case study, please contact Nathan B. George, deputy town manager, at 317/595-3117 or georgen@fishers.in.us.

City of Long Beach, CA

Case Profile

Population:
490,166

Square miles:
52

Median household income:
$43,746

Form of government:
Council-manager

Creating a culture of accountability

Many local governments struggle with the question of how to create—and sometimes strengthen—a culture of accountability within their organizations. A culture of accountability may include

- Establishing specific goals
- Linking these goals to strategic objectives
- Measuring progress toward goals
- Holding staff accountable and rewarding success.

City decides to stress accountability

The city of Long Beach is one community succeeding in the effort to embed a culture of accountability. Long known as an innovator in many areas of local government management, Long Beach has undertaken several deliberate efforts to promote its accountability culture:

- The city changed the name of its budget office to reflect the city's focus on performance and results (that is, accountability). Once known as the Budget Office, it is now the Budget and Performance Management Office.
- The city established a team of 13 performance coordinators who reside in each of the city's 13 city manager–led departments and who assist in the development, tracking, and reporting of performance information.
- In 2007 the city developed a monthly newsletter entitled *Performance News* that features news of the city's accountability efforts.

By highlighting the good work and successful management practices of different departments, newsletter staff seek to promote buy-in for the city's accountability efforts and to show the positive impact of performance management across the organization.

"Measure of the Month" focuses staff attention

To help keep employees focused on performance and accountability and expand their knowledge of how data are used to analyze results and drive strategy outside their own departments, the Budget and Performance Management Office developed *Performance News.* This monthly newsletter is distributed electronically to approximately 100 employees across the city, and hard copies are also posted in meeting areas and circulated at monthly administrative officer meetings and performance coordinator meetings. Each newsletter features:

- **City manager's message**—Each month, *Performance News* opens with a thematic message from the city manager supporting Long Beach's

For additional information about the practices described in this case study, please contact Sandra Palmer, administrative analyst, at sandra_palmer@longbeach.gov.

accountability efforts. (A number of ICMA Center for Performance Measurement™ [CPM] communities have noted that concrete, out-front support from the chief administrator is an essential component in building a performance-oriented culture.) The message includes

- Discussion of priorities and principles of good management
- Examples of how performance is used every day to drive strategy
- Goals for the current month.

- **Measure of the month**—Each month this column features information about one of the city's performance measures used to drive improvement in strategy and results. The column includes
  - Review of the relevant department's past performance on the measure
  - Strategies that were put in place to improve performance
  - Data demonstrating the desired improvement.

The city seeks to highlight a different department each month. By highlighting the good work and successful management practices of different departments, newsletter staff seek to promote buy-in for the city's accountability efforts and to show the positive impact of performance management across the organization.

Also provided in the newsletter is a monthly calendar. The calendar lists announcements, meetings, and deadlines related to the city's accountability programs.

City of North Las Vegas, NV

Case Profile

Population:
190,150

Square miles:
82

Median household income:
$53,183

Form of government:
Council-manager

Improving public reporting

The city of North Las Vegas was one of 19 local government organizations across North America to receive the new Government Performance Reporting Trailblazer Grant from the Center on Municipal Government Performance of the National Center for Civic Innovation (NCCI) for 2007. Three other winners in 2007 were also participants in the ICMA Center for Performance Measurement™ (CPM):

- City and county of Denver, Colorado
- City of Decatur, Georgia
- City of Vancouver, Washington.

New grant program supports public reporting improvements

NCCI's Web site states that the grant is intended "to encourage governments to involve the public in their performance measurement and reporting process and produce more accessible and engaging reports." Grantees may receive up to $12,500 to support efforts to gather citizen opinion regarding performance reports and improve such reports.

Grant-funded focus groups provide advice

The city of North Las Vegas used its grant award to conduct three citizen focus group meetings at which a facilitator presented segments of the city's most recent performance measurement report and sought feedback from participants. The report presented to the focus groups included

- CPM measures
- National Citizen Survey™ measures
- City-developed measures.

Two of the city's focus groups were conducted with English-speaking residents, and one was conducted with Spanish-speaking residents. City staff also worked to ensure that all major regions of the city were represented among the groups. Each group met for approximately two hours.

Suggestions that the focus groups made for improving North Las Vegas's next public performance report included:

- Add more descriptive data about the city to provide context for the performance information. (City staff noted that much of the descriptive information suggested by the focus groups is currently included in a separate annual report for citizens. Perhaps the reports will be folded together in the future.)
- Make the wording of the report accessible to wider audience; use less formal language.
- Add more graphics and pictures.

For additional information about the practices described in this case study, please contact Michelle Bailey-Hedgepeth, assistant to the city manager, at 702/633-1178 or baileyme@cityofnorthlasvegas.com.

The city of North Las Vegas plans to release a new performance report incorporating many of these suggestions in late 2008. It will be available through the city's Web site at www.cityofnorthlasvegas.com.

Network of grant winners is helpful, too

North Las Vegas staff noted that another benefit of the grant has been the ability to network with other grant-winning communities and share experiences with the public reporting of performance information. Grant winners travel to New York for group meetings twice during the year of their award.

City of Peoria, AZ

Case Profile

Population:
142,880

Square miles:
178

Median household income:
$61,657

Form of government:
Council-manager

Evolution of the use of performance measurement in a local government

The city of Peoria embarked upon performance measurement in 2000, developing measures and beginning to collect the corresponding data. The city then joined the ICMA Center for Performance Measurement™ (CPM) in FY 2005 and became a founding member of CPM's Arizona Performance Consortium that same year. (The consortium facilitates performance comparisons and effective practice research among CPM participants in the state of Arizona.)

Peoria started by presenting performance information in the annual budget

Since the city began collecting performance information in the early 2000s, it has used the data to inform budget decisions.

The city manager reminds department heads to rely no longer on telling a compelling story to back up their requests; they need to share compelling performance data.

In those early years of performance measurement implementation in Peoria, a number of departments began supplying their performance information with their annual budget requests, and many saw the rewards (in other words, they saw their requests approved) of justifying their requests with solid performance measurement backup data. The city also began sharing performance information in the annual budget document, which helped staff, elected officials, and citizens become comfortable with the presentation and use of this information.

City now houses performance data and budget data together, helping to demonstrate the link

As Peoria's performance measures and corresponding data became more reliable and robust in the mid-2000s, the city expanded its use of the data in budgeting and financial management processes.

In FY 2003, the city began tracking its performance data in the same computer system used to track its supplemental budget requests. The two types of information are tracked in separate modules, but housing the city's performance data with its budgetary information has helped to demonstrate the link between the two. The city plans to unite the two modules in the future, so that relevant performance measures and budgetary information may be even more directly linked.

The system is used to produce quarterly reports showing the city's progress against its budgetary and programmatic performance goals.

For additional information about the practices described in this case study, please contact Alex Munro, budget analyst, at 623/773-7146 or alex.munro@peoriaaz.gov.

Peoria will soon require performance data backup for all budget requests

Peoria began explicitly encouraging departments to use performance measurement data to justify supplemental budget requests with the FY 2006 budget process, and in FY 2008 the city directed departments to provide performance measurement backup data for supplemental requests wherever possible. In the upcoming years, the city plans to require backup data for all supplemental requests.

City staff note that supplemental requests related to programs required by state mandate, federal mandate, or other regulation will continue to be funded with or without backup information; however, these programs are encouraged to supply performance information whenever possible.

Engineering Department - Traffic Engineering

The Traffic Engineering Division ensures safe routes of transportation and improves the quality of life for Peoria residents through the establishment of traffic engineering standards, review of traffic impact studies and marking and signing plans, coordination of traffic counts, traffic investigations, preparation of school safe route plans, representation of City interests on various transportation committees (e.g., MAG ITS, AZTech, Valley Traffic Engineers Committee, etc.), coordination of the Neighborhood Traffic Management Program (NTMP), and by overseeing construction of traffic signals and proper traffic control for the City of Peoria.

Goals and Objectives

➢ **Improve traffic safety and quality of life for Peoria residents**	FY 2006 Budget	FY 2006 Actual	FY 2007 Projected
☒ Discourage unnecessary use of residential local and collector streets			
✓ Percent of NTMP projects resulting in measured decrease in speed of 10% or volume of 15%	85%	100%	90%
☒ Ensure Neighborhood Traffic Management Program (NTMP) projects are implemented in a timely manner and are consistent with City standards			
✓ Percent of NTMP projects implemented within 12 months of completed petition verification	80%	27%	50%
✓ Percent of projects with two or more features	85%	100%	85%

➢ **Create a safe school environment for Peoria students**	FY 2006 Budget	FY 2006 Actual	FY 2007 Projected
☒ Coordinate with Peoria school districts to provide new and updated Safe Route maps for each elementary school			
✓ Percent of elementary school Safe Route Maps created or updated within last 3 years	95%	100%	100%

➢ **Provide an efficient and corrdinated traffic signal system citywide**	FY 2006 Budget	FY 2006 Actual	FY 2007 Projected
☒ Study needs for new signals			
☒ Ensure that signals are in place where needed			
✓ Percent of warranted traffic signals installed	80%	65%	75%
☒ Revise and update existing signals and signal timing where needed			

Excerpt from Peoria's FY 2007 budget document showing performance measures for traffic engineering operations.

Council and manager rely on performance information to prioritize budget requests

During the budget approval process each year, all department heads present their supplemental requests to the city manager and the relevant deputy city manager. The department heads are required to prioritize their requests and are encouraged to provide performance measurement data to justify high-priority requests. City staff report anecdotally that department heads tend to be more successful in receiving allocations for requests backed up by hard performance data than for requests without such backup. Staff further note that the city manager reminds department heads to rely no longer on telling a compelling story to back up their requests; they need to share compelling performance data.

After receiving input from the city manager, department heads present their requests to the city council. Performance data are also shared with the councilmembers, and they use the data to inform their approvals.

County of Sarasota, FL

Robust, home-grown software promotes strategic management

GovMax is a Web-based application developed by Sarasota County that integrates strategic planning, business planning, performance management, and budgeting to help public sector agencies maximize performance, investments, and results. The only integrated system of its type designed specifically for government organizations, GovMax provides greater staff and technology efficiency, better accountability for the value of services delivered, and a more effective means of communicating outcomes to citizens.

Because managing organizational performance is in part everyone's responsibility, it is expected that people at all levels of the organization, from senior leaders to frontline staff, understand how the information in GovMax relates to them.

GovMax encourages a performance-oriented culture by linking contributions at the employee level with organization- and community-level objectives.

County staff are currently in the midst of updating the internally developed training program to meet the specific needs of different user groups. Power-user trainings have been developed for fiscal, strategic planning, and key administrative staff. Executive and managerial staff training focuses mostly on report generation and information summarization. Light-user training focuses on the concepts of strategy alignment and on where in the system users can go to find information that relates to goals and performance expectations relevant to them.

Spirit of collaboration

Sarasota County extended the use of GovMax to other local government and nonprofit agencies by offering the application and supporting technology through low-cost sharing agreements. For a small annual fee, other agencies can access a state-of-the-art system with no up-front costs; this means no software or hardware to purchase and no need for additional database administrators to manage the system.

Currently 17 partner organizations use the GovMax system. A major benefit to Sarasota County of this network of users is the cost-sharing arrangement among users that has allowed the county to recoup some of the development and maintenance costs associated with the system. Another benefit, no less important than the cost-sharing aspect, is the establishment of a diverse community of GovMax users. Community members exchange ideas about the software, its uses, and performance measurement generally. Topics discussed among users include approaches to strategic management, obstacles to implementing and sustaining a performance measurement system, and tips for performance measurement success.

Case Profile

Population:
367,867

Square miles:
620

Median household income:
$44,050

Form of government:
Council-administrator/manager

For additional information about the practices described in this case study, please contact Mary Sassi Furtado, executive director of strategic operations, at msassi@scgov.net.

Direct support of the strategic planning process

GovMax supports the strategic planning process by directly linking all budget items to one or more of the organization's strategic goals. The system

- Provides a tool to facilitate the execution of the strategy map
- Shows how key management processes affect the organization's balanced scorecard
- Aligns capital and operational expenses with relevant deliverables (in support of the organization's strategic goals)
- Encourages a performance-oriented culture by linking contributions at the employee level with organization- and community-level objectives.

Outcome-based budgeting

GovMax provides a service-based view of the budget as well as the more traditional department view. It allows for

- Alignment of people and business processes with the organization goals and objectives
- Links among expenditures, performance measures, and strategic actions
- Accountability at the employee level, enabling staff to take the right actions
- Coordination across organizational groups to help drive strategy execution.

Management efficiencies of GovMax

Sarasota County has also found that GovMax has boosted management efficiency by offering

- Compliance with higher information security mandates
- A 10-year horizon for both capital and operating budgets
- Fully integrated operating and capital modules that apply capital operation and maintenance impact automatically to the operating budget
- Fund transfer and balancing capability
- Budget splits at the employee level
- Quicker budget preparation capability, saving staff time and other resources
- An organizationwide application that eliminates the need to retrain employees on department-specific applications as they transfer within the organization
- A consistent reporting tool across the organization, from executive strategy to individual performance
- A comprehensive reporting capability that offers hundreds of different management reports that can be tailored independently by the casual user
- Document printing directly from the system.

City of University Place, WA

Case Profile

Population:
31,140

Square miles:
8

Median household income:
$54,782

Form of government:
Council-manager

Regional consortium comparisons and performance reports

The city of University Place joined the ICMA Center for Performance Measurement™ (CPM) in 2004. Along with 11 other local governments in the Seattle area, University Place helped form CPM's Puget Sound Consortium. CPM now offers 16 consortia, intended to enhance CPM participation for member governments by increasing opportunities for regional comparisons, information exchange, and peer support.

Performance memos inform many audiences

The city of University Place embarked on performance measurement in 1998 and has steadily refined its program over the years through actions like joining CPM (and its Puget Sound Consortium). One of the city's most recent improvements to its performance measurement program has been the introduction of regular "performance measurement memos" that feature analysis of the city's performance compared with neighboring communities in the Puget Sound Consortium. The goal of the memos is to promote understanding of University Place's strengths and weaknesses—and to identify opportunities to improve.

Addressed to the city's executive staff, the memos document the city's performance on measures of key interest to the city manager and city council. The memos are also presented to the city council at its regular meetings. Members of the public are informed about the memos through public broadcast of the city council meetings, distribution of the memos at the city council meetings, and on-request distribution of the memos at city hall.

Consortium core measures facilitate relevant comparisons

The memos feature information about the city's performance on the Puget Sound Consortium's "core measures." Each CPM consortium selects a set of core measures from among all of the performance measures offered through CPM. (Some core measures may also be developed independently by consortium members.) These core measures represent the service areas and specific pieces of performance information that consortium members deem most relevant for regional comparison and effective practice research; consortium members commit to one another that they will collect and submit data for these measures.

For each consortium core measure, the performance measurement memos include a graph and written explanation of the data; the graphs show all jurisdictions in the consortium. These consortium graphs add regional context to the city's performance information—boosting clarity and relevance for staff and residents.

For additional information about the practices described in this case study, please contact Lisa Petorak, human resources manager/management analyst, at lpetorak@cityofup.com.

City of Vancouver, WA

Case Profile

Population:
156,600

Square miles:
50

Median household income:
$40,743

Form of government:
Council-manager

Representing the opinions of all residents-English speakers and non-English speakers alike

Vancouver has been one of the highest-growth cities in Washington State for a number of years, owing in great part to immigration.

Surveying both English speakers and non-English speakers provides fuller picture of resident opinion

As part of Vancouver's FY 2007–2008 strategic plan update, city officials wanted to gather opinions about city services from all residents—regardless of their English-language knowledge. Previously, Vancouver's strategic planning survey and biannual citizen survey had been conducted only in English. City officials were concerned that continuing with an English-only survey format might not generate a complete picture of resident opinion across the city. Thus, the city decided to conduct its 2007 survey in multiple languages.

City leadership felt this was an innovative effort that allowed the city to obtain information otherwise unavailable.

The city undertook research with its existing foreign-language translation contractor to determine which languages in addition to English would be most useful for a resident survey. City officials also consulted census data and other community resources as part of their research. The research indicated that Korean, Russian, and Spanish were the most common languages among Vancouver residents (after English).

Translation costs may be lower than you think

The city enlisted its regular translation contractor to convert its English-language survey into the three foreign-language versions for only $100 per language. The simple, one-page survey was distributed in hard copy through community organizations such as culture clubs, churches, and community support organizations that work with foreign-language-speaking residents who use the target languages. A number of English-language-learner classes at the local community college presented the survey as an in-class assignment and assisted in basic analysis of the results. Online versions of the foreign-language surveys were also created and made available through the Web-based, commercial survey service, SurveyMonkey™.

Only about 100–200 responses to the foreign-language surveys were expected, but Vancouver received more than 550 responses—the majority on paper. Representatives from each foreign-language group assisted with the translation of the written responses, which not only helped keep translation costs low but also boosted community support for the effort. This was the

For additional information about the practices described in this case study, please contact Tom Nosack, performance analyst, at tom.nosack@ci.vancouver.wa.us.

first time the city of Vancouver received such high levels of survey participation from residents who are not native speakers of English.

Here is a sampling of responses from Vancouver's foreign-language surveys:

- **How can we help you feel more involved?**—28 percent of respondents indicated that they would like city officials to listen and communicate more with them.
- **How can the city government help you feel more involved? What can we change?**—One respondent wrote, "We moved here four years ago. We have since been very active in two neighborhood associations and have testified about critical development issues in front of the city council. My voice was never valued much [where we lived previously], yet in Vancouver, I feel that the public opinion is heard, considered, and respected."
- **Other feedback**—Another respondent wrote, "I just wanted to thank you again for working with the ESL program. Reading the update of the strategic plan made me feel that the voices of our students were truly heard—it made me proud to say that I live in Vancouver!"

The response to Vancouver's effort has been interesting and rewarding. Vancouver has learned that

- First-generation immigrants who have difficulty with English will respond to surveys brought to them at a place comfortable to them as a group and provided in their native language
- If new immigrants are Internet savvy and have the option to take a survey online, they will almost always take a survey in English, not their native language
- Surveyed citizens were very appreciative and want the city to continue asking for their input
- Citizens who participated in collecting and reviewing the data were energized about their role in the survey
- This innovative effort allowed the city to obtain information otherwise unavailable, and the surveys affected the city of Vancouver's strategic plan update.
- The city council, impressed with the effort, can now take this important part of overall citizen opinion and respond to this group more fully than it had in the past.

A complete review of the results of this effort is available at www.cityofvancouver.us/StrategicPlan.

City of Westminster, CO

Case Profile

Population:
109,671

Square miles:
34

Median household income:
$67,094

Form of government:
Council-manager

How to cultivate a learning model and team approach to performance measurement

To ensure that Westminster's performance measurement efforts constitute a management tool and not just a data collection exercise, Westminster's city manager requires department heads to submit annual performance reports, and he has staffed and trained a team of professionals to support the effort (in concert with their other duties).

Performance measurement is not merely a data collection exercise, but rather a management practice to understand, justify, and improve operations. We must focus our efforts and measure what really matters.

The reports are required to go beyond simple lists of inputs and outputs. They must include analysis of progress toward outcomes and explanations of different aspects of service delivery performance. Moreover, the reports are used not to expose and punish shortcomings but to highlight areas for improvement and seek solutions.

For a recent reporting cycle, city manager Brent McFall asked department heads to address the following questions in their performance reports:

- How do this year's performance measures reflect progress toward the strategic plan goals and objectives?
- What are notable trends, exemplary accomplishments and achievements, and areas for improvement?
- How have performance measures been used to evaluate and direct operations during the year? How have performance measures been used to make improvements or validate current practices?
- How has performance measurement been integrated into your department?

Department heads receive assistance from Westminster's citywide performance measurement team in drafting their reports. The team is composed of staff members from each department who act as champions for performance measurement efforts within each department. Team members receive special training in performance measurement philosophy and practice and are available to provide subject matter expertise and analytical support within their departments—to both department heads and fellow staff.

The city manager and performance measurement team review each department's report in detail. The reports are then used in three ways:

- To make operational changes, where appropriate
- To assemble for the city council the annual performance report, *Take a Closer Look: How Performance Measures Build a Better City,* which highlights progress toward internal targets and comparisons with peer

To learn more about the practices described in the case study, please contact Aric Otzelberger at 303/658-2400 or aotzelberger@ci.westminster.co.us.

communities (drawn from ICMA Center for Performance Measurement™ [CPM] data) in a digest format (and provides feedback from the city's biennial citizen survey in even-numbered years)

- To assess each departments' utilization—and understanding—of performance measurement in day-to-day operations.

A major goal of this process is to foster understanding of performance measurement—not simply to go through the motions of the practice. In fact, to ensure that department heads "walk the talk," the city manager also discusses the use and application of performance measures within department operations during employees' individual appraisals.

The city manager asserts, "When examining our performance measures, we must ask ourselves, 'So what?' Performance measurement is not merely a data collection exercise, but rather a management practice to understand, justify, and improve operations. We must focus our efforts and measure what really matters."

City of Woodbury, MN

Case Profile

Population:
57,024

Square miles:
36

Median household income:
$76,109

Form of government:
Mayor-council

Cross-training police personnel as paramedics and firefighters

The city of Woodbury recognized in the mid-1990s that in order to meet the increasing public safety needs of its growing population without breaking the bank, it would need to consider some creative staffing options. In 1995, the city began cross-training some police officers as paramedics, and in 1996 it merged its fire and emergency medical services (EMS) with its police service.

By 2004 it became clear, however, that additional measures were needed to ensure continued provision of robust public safety services within the city's existing financial constraints. A major concern at the time was that the city's pool of paid, on-call volunteer firefighters had not grown with the city's population. From 1991 to 2005, the city's population had increased by 275 percent while the number of paid, on-call volunteers had remained static.

Woodbury expects to see cost savings compared with traditional fire staffing models, improved response times, and the preservation of lives and property.

Although the city of Woodbury was in a relatively strong financial position in 2004, it did not have the money to add the number of regular, full-time firefighters that would have been needed to make up for the shortage in the paid, on-call volunteer pool. Moreover, the city was also concerned that, with its growing population, a shortage of police officers might become a problem.

Consider all options

To address these concerns, the city in late 2004 formed a fire-EMS task force comprising citizens, elected officials, and city staff. The task force was charged with drafting recommendations for public safety service standards and performance measures that represented community expectations. Task force members also recommended staffing levels to meet the new service standards.

The task force considered a number of different public safety organizational models and ultimately recommended the public safety integration model, which features the cross-training of public safety personnel in multiple disciplines. A major benefit of the model was considered to be the likelihood of improving fire response times because on-duty police officers are usually among the first to respond to an emergency; under the new model many police officers would be cross-trained as firefighters. Task force members also noted that the recommended model would cost less than implementing a traditional, full-time fire service. In addition, the task force recommended the hiring of additional public safety personnel to meet growing service demands in both police and fire.

Gain employee buy-In

The city recognized that in order for implementation of the new model to be successful, public safety employees would have to support the change. The

i

For additional information about the practices described in this case study, please contact Matthew Stemwedel, administration analyst, at mstemwedel@ci.woodbury.mn.us.

city began its effort to ensure employee support by surveying public safety staff, asking them, "What makes you the best at what you do?" and "What would it take to get better?" To boost the likelihood of generating candid responses, the survey was anonymous.

Nearly 80 percent of staff members returned the survey. Results indicated that the employees had some concerns about communication among the different public safety disciplines and staffing levels.

Develop a plan

Public safety supervisors met in a two-day retreat to develop responses to the concerns raised in the employee survey. Four months later, another retreat for all public safety staff was held; it came to be called the "Big Meeting." Strategies for implementing the new organization model were discussed under the overall question, "What will it take for us to move from good to great?" Obstacles were identified, solutions were proposed, and an action plan was created.

Execute the plan

Woodbury's public safety department set the action plan into motion a few weeks after the Big Meeting.

Under the terms of the action plan, current police officers were encouraged to pursue cross-training as firefighters or paramedics, and new officers were required to receive cross-training in one discipline or the other. During 2007 and 2008, all police command staff and 10 police officers were trained as firefighters; they now respond to both police and fire calls during their shifts. New police officers are cross-trained as firefighters or paramedics.

Since implementing the new organizational model, the department has been able to streamline other processes. Some time-consuming paperwork has been reduced by eliminating a redundant dispatching system and creating a new standby system for remaining paid, on-call volunteer firefighters. To better coordinate building inspections, fire inspection services were transferred from the fire division to the inspection services division of Woodbury's community development department.

Monitor performance over time

Implementation of its new organizational model has allowed Woodbury to streamline and improve its public safety services. With many of the changes less than one year old, the city looks forward to collecting and reviewing performance data to assess the effectiveness of these changes over time.

Woodbury expects to see cost savings compared with traditional fire staffing models, improved response times, and the preservation of lives and property. Performance will be tracked by budgetary measures, established benchmarks, annual employee satisfaction surveys, and biennial citizen satisfaction surveys.

Report results

Results will be reported in the city's annual performance measurement report and budget document. Data drawn from the city's participation in the ICMA Center for Performance Measurement™ (CPM) are displayed in Woodbury's annual performance measurement report, and the data show the city's performance compared with its peers. The CPM indicator "response time in minutes to top priority calls" is one that is featured in the city's report.

Code Enforcement

Code Enforcement

City of Dallas, TX

Performance Indicators

- **Average number of calendar days from case initiation to voluntary compliance**
- **Average number of calendar days from case initiation to administrative/judicial action**

During FY 2005 and FY 2006, the city of Dallas reported that it was able to reduce the average time from case initiation to voluntary compliance for all violation types from 28 days to 11 days. The mean time required to achieve voluntary compliance for all jurisdictions reporting in FY 2006 was 36 days; the median was 15 days.

The average time from case initiation to administrative/judicial action as reported by Dallas for FY 2006 was five days. The mean and median values for all jurisdictions reporting were 39 days and 31 days, respectively.

When asked how the city had been able to achieve these performance levels, Dallas's code enforcement officer cited four major factors:

- Adaptation to the city's relatively new customer relationship management system (CRMS)
- Enhanced ability to track open cases
- Establishment of time standards for resolving cases
- Introduction of civil adjudication process.

New CRMS presented some challenges

The city implemented a new CRMS in 2002, and some time was required to

- Assess the capabilities of the system
- Educate staff about how to use the system
- Write computer programs to generate the most useful reports possible from the system.

New system boosted case-tracking abilities

Despite the initial challenges, the CRMS offered many features beyond the city's previous code enforcement computer system. Perhaps the most important of these was the ability to monitor cases at every point in the inspection and resolution process rather than simply report the case initiation and closure dates.

Case tracking led to customer service standards—and enhanced responsiveness

With the new ability to track cases at each stage of the inspection process, the city was able to

- Calculate average time frames for resolving past cases
- Determine optimal time frames for resolving future cases.

Case Profile

Population:
1,260,950

Square miles:
385

Median household income:
$36,403

Form of government:
Council-manager

For additional information about the practices described in this case study, please contact Bob Curry, code enforcement officer, at robert.curry@dallascityhall.com.

Inspectors are now held accountable for ensuring that each step in the inspection process is completed within a standard time frame.

The system also informs managers of cases that remain open fourteen and seven days from their case closure deadlines, so that managers may check in with inspectors about such cases. This system has helped reduce response time considerably.

To enhance customer service further by "closing the loop" with customers who initiate cases, the CRMS now automatically notifies the initiator of a case—by mail or e-mail, depending on the method that was used to initiate the case—when the case is closed.

Introduction of civil adjudication process helped reduce time required in administrative/judicial cases

The city also recently introduced a civil adjudication process to promote quicker resolution of some code violation cases that could not be resolved by voluntary compliance or the regular citation process. Previously, all cases that could not be handled by these two options had to be referred to criminal court, which was frequently a very time-consuming process. Moreover, the inspector was required to testify about such cases in person, thus taking time that could have been spent working on cases in the field.

Under the city's new civil process, less serious cases requiring court intervention may be heard in civil court, which has shorter wait times than criminal court. Another benefit is that the inspector is not required to appear in person; the inspector may submit testimony through written reports and photographs.

On-board, wireless computers may boost performance further

The city is in the process of equipping all inspectors' vehicles with wireless computers so that they may enter data, issue citations, and conduct other business directly from the field. This is expected to save additional time that some inspectors must spend traveling to a city office and entering case data there. (Some inspectors already have mobile data terminals that permit some data entry in the field.)

ICMA-CPM participation encourages frequent reporting and analysis of performance data

Dallas's code enforcement officer also noted that, among other motivators, the city's participation in the ICMA Center for Performance Measurement™ (CPM) has encouraged frequent reporting and analysis of performance information. Different complements of information are reported daily, monthly, and annually. He noted that city staff present Dallas's code enforcement performance as compared with peer communities in CPM every year, and they seek reasons for differences in order to promote further improvement in their performance.

City of Moorhead, MN

Performance Indicator

- **Average number of calendar days from case initiation to voluntary compliance**

For FY 2006, the city of Moorhead reported an average number of six calendar days from case initiation to voluntary compliance. The mean and median values for all jurisdictions reporting were 36 and 15, respectively.

Encourage voluntary compliance with clear expectations

Although all residential and commercial properties in the city of Moorhead are subject to code enforcement, the majority of Moorhead's code inspections are on rental properties connected with the three colleges located within the city limits.

The city's neighborhood services division requires that all rental properties be inspected once a year by its rental registration and inspection unit. The unit comprises a full-time rental-housing code technician, two building inspectors (who assist during off-peak building construction periods), and several firefighters (who assist during two blitz inspection periods each year).

By informing rental-property owners of expectations and penalties in advance of their annual inspections, Moorhead has enjoyed a great deal of success in boosting voluntary compliance with checklist items and citations issued during inspections.

Routine rental-housing inspections are scheduled in advance. Code violations in rental properties may be addressed on an ad hoc basis as complaints are received.

Prior to a routine rental-property inspection, the city sends to the property owner a detailed preinspection checklist and a list of fees that may be assessed if a reinspection is required or if a violation is found and not remedied. Property owners are asked to use the checklist as a guide to ensure that their properties will pass the initial inspection. If a reinspection is required, the fee is $100. If a code violation is found and not corrected within a prescribed time period, penalty fees range from $100 to $2,000 per violation.

By informing rental-property owners of expectations and penalties in advance of their annual inspections, Moorhead has enjoyed a great deal of success in boosting voluntary compliance with checklist items and citations issued during inspections. In the first full year of instituting the $100 reinspection fee (previously, the first reinspection was free), the city experienced an 85 percent decrease in its reinspection rate.

Identify and educate property owners

To identify unregistered property owners—and make sure they receive their preinspection notices—Moorhead's code enforcement staff patrol the city

Case Profile

Population:
34,244

Square miles:
19

Median household income:
$34,781

Form of government:
Council-manager

For additional information about the practices described in this case study, please contact Lisa Vatnsdal, neighborhood services manager, at lisa.vatnsdal@cityofmoorhead.com.

for rental signs, peruse the real estate section of the newspaper, and cross-check their findings against registered properties and city tax rolls. Failure to register a rental property results in a $100 fine.

The city of Moorhead also operates a crime-free housing landlord education program wherein property owners are taught about fair housing regulations, crime prevention, property management, and applicable city codes. Attendance at this class is required within six months of registration for new landlords. By teaching landlords about what is required of them, the city speculates that it may be preventing many code violations.

Apply administrative instead of criminal penalties when possible

When voluntary compliance cannot be achieved, the city of Moorhead has the approval of the Clay County district court to apply civil penalties for nuisance, property maintenance, and zoning violations. This civil process allows quicker resolution of less serious but hard-to-resolve cases than the criminal process would. To ensure preservation of violators' due process rights, Moorhead's civil adjudication process incorporates appeal and judicial review provisions.

Organize staff to maximize efficiency and effectiveness

To ensure that all cases are addressed in a timely manner, in 2005 the city of Moorhead reorganized its code enforcement staff. The neighborhood services division merged its own inspection staff with inspection staff that were previously housed in the fire department. This change encouraged a more holistic approach to property inspections, and it also boosted inspector efficiency. (Firefighters still independently inspect larger, multifamily apartment complexes, however.)

Each week, members of the city's code enforcement staff meet to discuss any emerging trends in code enforcement activities in the city and address open or overlapping cases. This enables staff to reinforce the community development philosophy of the division.

Staff in the code enforcement division also attribute much of their success in achieving high rates of voluntary compliance and other code enforcement triumphs to the support of the city council. The council has upheld penalties and suspensions of rental registration when documented efforts to bring properties into compliance have not been heeded by property owners. Neighborhood residents have also been strong supporters of the division's efforts.

Moorhead's city code may be found on its Web site (www.cityofmoorhead.com). The rental registration program is included in Chapter 9-7. The administrative citations and civil penalties structure is included in Chapter 1-4-4.

City of Palm Coast, FL

Performance Indicator

- **Average number of calendar days from case initiation to initiation of administrative/judicial process**

For FY 2006, the city of Palm Coast reported that the average time from case initiation to initiation of the administrative/judicial process was 42 calendar days. Although Palm Coast's performance was close to the mean and median values of 39 calendar days and 31 calendar days, respectively, for all jurisdictions reporting, the city had reduced its cycle time from 137 calendar days in FY 2005 to 42 calendar days in FY 2006.

Organize for success

One major factor contributing to Palm Coast's success in reducing its cycle time so greatly between FY 2005 and FY 2006 was that, leading into FY 2006, the city appointed a new person to serve as its building official. The new building official was an internal hire who first began working for the city as a code enforcement officer in 2004. Because of his knowledge of the city's code enforcement program and commitment to the city's mission, the new building official was able to streamline code enforcement procedures and reorganize the department quickly to address concerns about cycle times and other issues.

The city's code enforcement division is now responsible for all building and code enforcement. The division inspects improvements in residential and nonresidential developments, issues building permits, and performs inspections during construction. The department also maintains responsibility for investigating complaints of code violations, inspecting commercial properties for code compliance, and providing information to the city council as well as certain boards and commissions of the city.

Expedite hearings

The code enforcement board of the city of Palm Coast also plays a pivotal role in the city's success in keeping cycle times as short as possible. The board meets monthly to review cases, which helps to promote good cycle times by preventing a backlog of cases requiring board action. The board also seeks to move quickly through cases, to minimize further the number of calendar days that each case remains open.

The board includes, whenever possible, an architect, a businessperson, an engineer, a general contractor, a subcontractor, and a realtor—who in combination provide the expertise necessary to dispose of cases quickly.

At its hearings, the board has the authority to subpoena alleged violators, witnesses, and evidence; take testimony under oath; and issue force-of-the-law orders that command the steps necessary to bring a violation into compliance. With the goal of promoting, protecting, and improving the health, safety, and welfare of the citizens of Palm Coast, the board also has the authority to impose administrative fines and other noncriminal penalties

Case Profile

Population:
71,076

Square miles:
64

Median household income:
$45,175

Form of government:
Council-manager

For additional information about the practices described in this case study, please contact Gary Bunting, performance measures management analyst, at gbunting@ci.palm-coast.fl.us.

promoting equitable, expeditious, effective, and inexpensive methods of enforcing codes and ordinances in effect in the city.

Establish meaningful measures

To ensure their relevance, the city of Palm Coast has aligned its code enforcement performance standards with its community development goals. To this end, the city's first code enforcement performance standard requires that code violations be documented and processed within 24 hours of being reported to the city. A second standard is that staff-initiated code enforcement cases must exceed the number of citizen-initiated cases. The goal of the second standard is to encourage proactive code enforcement, with the intent being that code enforcement officers assess and respond to code violations before they become major problems. To achieve this proactive enforcement goal, code enforcement officers patrol 100 percent of their zones at least twice a month.

Promote accountability

The city of Palm Coast uses ManagePro, a commercial software package, to collect its performance data. The software captures data for all custom city measures and many ICMA Center for Performance Measurement™ (CPM) measures. Results are then reported monthly to the city manager and council. The city manager gauges progress toward the council's strategic goals largely from these reports as well as from citizen survey results and other customer feedback.

The city's performance measurement software will eventually allow the linking of the city's strategic plan goals to individual employee goals, which should help show employees the responsibility and influence that they have on the city's efforts to improve services.

Department managers already participate in the city manager's annual performance review, where they report on the efforts of their individual departments to advance the city's strategic goals.

The city also has a dedicated performance measurement team. Each department has a representative on the team. Team members periodically receive training designed to sharpen data collection skills and help generate enthusiasm among fellow employees for reporting accurate performance data.

Facilities Management

Facilities Management

City of Bellevue, WA

Performance Indicators

- **Overall satisfaction with custodial service**
- **Timeliness of repair service**

For FY 2006, the city of Bellevue's facilities management division reported that 88 percent of its customers rated overall satisfaction with custodial service as excellent or good. The mean and median values for all jurisdictions reporting were 69 percent and 68 percent, respectively.

On the timeliness of repair service, 92 percent of Bellevue's customers gave a rating of excellent or good. The mean value for all jurisdictions reporting was 87 percent, and the median value was 90 percent.

In February 2006, the city of Bellevue moved into a new city hall with approximately twice the square footage of its previous facility. Although the newness of the facility may have helped boost customer satisfaction, city staff suggest that changes in space utilization and service response patterns have also positively affected customer satisfaction ratings and helped the city keep energy costs relatively consistent with costs at the previous facility.

Location, location, location—and relocation

In connection with the opening of the new city hall, several offices previously housed in separate locations were consolidated at the new building. The police department, for example, used to have just a small contingent of staff at city hall. Now all administrative, records, custody, patrol, and detective staff are based there, along with regional 911 staff. Some fire administration staff members have also moved to city hall. These consolidations have improved information technology efficiency and communication between the departments.

Another significant relocation was that of the facilities maintenance staff itself. With most of the city's square footage concentrated at city hall, Bellevue found it made more sense for the facilities staff to be based there rather than at its previous off-site location. This put the facilities staff closer to its major customer base, and it improved response times for repair requests for most customers. (The opening of the new city hall also reduced from seven to four the number of buildings that in-house and contract facilities staff maintain.)

Consolidation of custodial services saved 15 percent

With 24-hour public safety operations now being housed in city hall and more square footage to be cleaned, Bellevue's facilities maintenance division realized that custodial services needed to be changed. Thus, the city issued a request for proposals for all city hall custodial services, including window cleaning, carpet cleaning, and restroom maintenance. Previously handled by several vendors, these services under the new arrangement were consolidated with one vendor. In addition, some services (for example, collection of office trash) that were once provided every other day were changed to daily service.

Case Profile

Population:
117,000

Square miles:
32

Median household income:
$69,880

Form of government:
Council-manager

For additional information about the practices described in this case study, please contact Rich Siegel, performance and outreach coordinator, at rcsiegel@bellevuewa.gov.

The consolidation resulted in enhanced services for customers and a 15 percent reduction in custodial service costs per square foot.

New building saves energy—and money

The design of the new building offers a number of improvements compared with the previous building, including enhanced security features like keycard access to office areas and greater energy efficiency. Moreover, the energy-saving measures have promoted cost savings, too.

Although square footage in the new building effectively doubled the footage of the old building, the implementation of energy-saving technology has kept the utility costs of the new building reasonably consistent compared with the older building.

Energy-saving technologies implemented in the new city hall building include

- High efficiency boilers and chillers
- Upgraded building control system
- Variable frequency drive additions
- Under-floor heating, ventilation, and air conditioning ducts
- Day lighting approach (window wall sensors for dimming and automatic shutoff)
- Exterior building cladding to ensure good insulation.

Ongoing energy savings of $70,000 annually are anticipated owing to implementation of these technologies, which have already garnered Bellevue a rebate grant of $165,000 from the local utility provider, Puget Sound Energy.

Actively seek feedback

Facilities maintenance staff conduct regular meetings and annual customer survey feedback discussion sessions with representatives of each department to ensure that custodial and repair operations meet the needs of the jurisdiction staff. In these meetings, facilities managers review prior results, custodial services, HVAC issues, and any other department concerns.

Look for trends and schedule accordingly

Recognizing the many functions that city hall serves, schedulers in the division have adjusted custodial service schedules to meet customers' needs. Although most custodial services are provided after-hours in Bellevue, a new "day porter" is now available to respond to special event needs or emergency requests as they arise.

With a number of meeting facilities available on the first two floors of the building, the facility sometimes functions as a mini conference center. As such, some staff have been assigned to swing shifts or even Saturday shifts to handle the special events. Also, after-hours and weekend security staff have been added.

City of Charlottesville, VA

Performance Indicator

- **Electricity expenditures per square foot for administrative/office facilities**

For FY 2006, the city of Charlottesville, Virginia, reported spending $1.58 per square foot for electricity in administrative/office facilities. The mean and median values reported for all jurisdictions were $0.32 and $0.07 respectively.

Reviewing data prompts meaningful questions

While reviewing performance data from the city's participation in the ICMA Center for Performance Measurement™ (CPM), Charlottesville's facilities maintenance manager noticed that the city was paying significantly more for electricity than other local governments in the state. With the hope that their techniques might be applicable to his operation, he decided to contact some of these in-state peers to find out how they were keeping their costs lower than Charlottesville's.

As [the facilities maintenance manager] recounts, he picked up the phone and reached out: "My question was, 'Okay, how did you do it?' Then, I shut up and listened and learned."

Charlottesville's facilities maintenance manager, using the participant contact search feature on CPM's private Web site, found contact information for his counterparts in neighboring communities. As he recounts, he then picked up the phone and reached out: "My question was, 'Okay, how did you do it?' Then, I shut up and listened and learned."

Questions lead to money-saving solutions

From his phone calls, Charlottesville's facilities maintenance manager found out that some of his lower-paying peers were using a technique called load shedding to reduce the cost per kilowatt hour that they were being charged by the local electric utility.

The local utility company bases the rate that a customer pays for each kilowatt hour throughout the year on the amount of energy consumed in the customer's highest-demand half hour during the June–September time frame. The more energy that is consumed during this highest-demand half hour, the higher the rate that the customer is charged throughout the year. The utility company explained that this rate structure allows it to maintain the capacity necessary to meet the customer's highest demand for electricity.

Electricity load-shedding solution is projected to save $350,000 per year

With load shedding, customers reduce electricity consumption strategically throughout the day to avoid the peaks that result in the application of higher

Case Profile

Population:
40,745

Square miles:
10

Median household income:
$31,007

Form of government:
Council-manager

For additional information about the practices described in this case study, please contact Lance Stewart, facilities maintenance manager, at 434/970-3665 or STEWARTL@charlottesville.org.

rates by the electricity provider. To gauge whether load shedding would save money in Charlottesville, the facilities maintenance manager identified two large, almost identical buildings (both schools) for a load-shedding trial.

Charlottesville had the advantage of already having climate automation systems in these buildings that permitted detailed tracking of energy consumption. The systems also included the programming necessary to shed electricity load based on consumption patterns. Staff determined the peak consumption hours for the two buildings and instituted load-shedding strategies at those peak times. These strategies, which were set up to not exceed the prescribed maximum indoor summer temperatures for these buildings, included

- Raising the cooling temperature set point on individual air handlers in sequence throughout the peak demand period
- Allowing walk-in freezers to sit without cooling power for a few minutes periodically during the peak demand periods.

This trial resulted in a 12 percent rate reduction, which translates to an impressive $16,321 annual savings to the city for these two buildings alone.

After the city of Charlottesville realized such robust cost savings from its two-building trial, the facilities maintenance staff decided to apply the load-shedding system to all of the buildings for which it is responsible. When all buildings are finally included, the city projects an annual savings of 10 percent—approximately $350,000.

County of James City, VA

Performance Indicator

- **Overall customer satisfaction with custodial service**

For FY 2006, James City County reported that 94.4 percent of customers rated custodial services as excellent or good. For all jurisdictions reporting that year, the mean and median proportions of these responses were 69.3 percent and 67.7 percent, respectively.

When asked how the county promotes such high customer satisfaction with custodial services, county staff cited the following factors:

- Ensuring continuous provision of custodial services, regardless of regular staff availability
- Shifting workloads strategically when staff shortages occur
- Holding staff accountable for providing good service.

Provide high-quality, uninterrupted service

To ensure that good custodial service can be provided even when a regular staff member is ill, on vacation, or otherwise unable to work, James City County has implemented an on-call custodian program. When a regular staff member is unable to work, one of the county's four on-call custodians is called to cover the shift. The county provides its on-call custodians with the same training as its regular staff members to ensure that high-quality service is provided regardless of whether the work is done by a regular or an on-call custodian. On-call custodians are paid only for the hours they work, so the program represents a low-cost solution to the challenge of providing continuous, high-quality service to customers.

In the rare instance that an on-call custodian is not available to fill in for a regular staff member who is out, the remaining custodians prioritize their work to ensure that, among all areas needing to be served, the highest-use and highest-traffic areas receive attention first. One example of a high-priority area is the locker rooms at the county's community center during the morning and evening rush periods. By focusing on areas that are most valued by customers, the custodial staff is able to emphasize its commitment to meeting customer needs.

Hold staff accountable for high-quality service

James City County's custodial staff also keeps checklists in all county restrooms; on these checklists custodians record the times and types of services performed throughout the day. Although many organizations do this, James City County takes the checklists one step further: it uses them as a feedback tool for the staff. The lead custodian reviews the checklists and thus ensures that required tasks are performed, the quality of the work is high, and staff understand what was done well and what could be done better.

The checklists also provide a common benchmark for the staff, communicating the message that everyone is on the same team and, by working together to the same standard, the team can provide the highest-quality service. In

Case Profile

Population:
56,600

Square miles:
176

Median household income:
$62,271

Form of government:
Council-administrator

For additional information about the practices described in this case study, please contact Grace Boone at 757/259-4082 or at gboone@james-city.va.us.

addition, the lists not only promote accountability for custodial staff but also demonstrate accountability to the customers who see them.

Manage service requests efficiently

To ensure that customers' ad hoc custodial maintenance needs are met in a timely fashion, James City County established a network of building coordinators to help process custodial maintenance requests. Each county building has a building coordinator who is a regular county employee charged with receiving and submitting to the facilities maintenance office any requests for things like spill cleanup and light-bulb replacement. The building coordinators enter their requests through an online system.

When the request is received by the maintenance office, a work order is created and an estimated completion date for the request is recorded. Having a single point of contact for such requests within each building eliminates duplicate requests for service and improves communication about the status of a request.

Building coordinators maintain responsibility for informing building occupants about progress on service requests. This worked particularly well in one situation where the air conditioning unit in a building broke down: Through the building coordinator, the maintenance office was able to provide building occupants with hourly updates. Without the building coordinator, the maintenance office might have been inundated with calls for information about when the repair would be complete, stymieing employees' ability to respond to that service problem and others as efficiently as possible.

Seek customer feedback and apply results

James City County's facilities maintenance staff noted that it surveys customers each year in order to identify its priorities for the upcoming year. The county also noted that it used data from its participation in the ICMA Center for Performance Measurement™ (CPM) to compare its own performance with that of peer communities.

Town of Queen Creek, AZ

Performance Indicator

- **Overall customer satisfaction with custodial service**

For 2006, the town of Queen Creek reported that 100 percent of customers rated the overall quality of custodial service as excellent or good. The mean and median proportions reported by all jurisdictions were 69 percent and 68 percent, respectively.

Queen Creek's facilities manager noted four key factors in satisfying customers of the town's custodial service operation:

- Recruitment for a positive attitude in new employees
- Increase in the work morale of current employees
- Adherence to the philosophy of "inspect for what you expect"
- Provision of opportunities for custodial staff to interact with customers.

Among new recruits, attitude sometimes trumps skills

The facilities manager noted that, although he is usually able to teach the skills necessary to perform custodial services well, he finds it difficult to cultivate a positive attitude in people who do not have one. Thus, he recruits first for attitude and second for skill. Employees with a positive attitude tend to perform their work better as well as interact with customers in a more positive way.

High staff morale promotes customer satisfaction

The facilities manager also noted that although a positive attitude at the beginning is important, he seeks to keep morale high by

- **Offering enhanced work opportunities when possible**—In one case where the manager needed to respond to a growing workload, he was able to offer full-time status to three part-time employees instead of hiring additional part-time employees.
- **Encouraging employees to pursue professional certifications**—All five of the town's custodians hold custodian certificates through the Cleaning Management Institute; some are also pursuing the institute's supervisory certificate.

Inspect for what you expect

Queen Creek's custodial staff operate with the philosophy: inspect for what you expect. In other words, create the environment that pleases you—and your customers.

Custodial staff interact with and respond to customers

The facilities manager encourages members of the custodial staff to interact with customers, and he schedules their work to allow time for such interaction. While many organizations schedule custodial work during hours when most customers are not present, the town of Queen Creek schedules all

Case Profile

Population:
22,477

Square miles:
26

Median household income:
$63,702

Form of government:
Council-manager

For additional information about the practices described in this case study, please contact Lee Councilor, facilities manager, at lee.councilor@queencreek.org.

custodians to work at least part of their day when customers occupy their offices; the custodial staff work staggered schedules between 5:00 a.m. and 6:00 p.m.

Little things—like hand soap—mean a lot

One of the most popular results of such interaction with customers was a change in hand soap used in town bathroom facilities. The town had been stocking an institutional soap product available through its regular cleaning supply vendor. When talking with a custodial staff member one day, another town staff member asked whether it would be possible to switch to a commercially available hand soap with a different scent.

The custodian checked with the facilities manager who determined that the commercial soap was no more expensive than the institutional product. The commercial soap was introduced, and customer feedback has been overwhelming and positive. Moreover, the change—and positive customer response—might not have occurred without the informal interactions encouraged by a friendly and available custodial staff.

City of Reno, NV

Performance Indicator

- **Customer satisfaction with timeliness of repair service**

For FY 2006, Reno reported that 94 percent of customers rated the timeliness of facilities maintenance repair services as excellent or good. The mean and median values for all jurisdictions reporting were 87 percent and 90 percent, respectively.

When asked how the city achieved such good ratings for timeliness of repairs, Reno's facilities maintenance manager cited three factors:

- Geographic assignment of technicians
- Aggressive preventive maintenance program
- Real-time, online service request system.

This system has not only boosted the convenience for these employees, who no longer have to wait on the phone to request maintenance assistance; it has also improved maintenance staff efficiency by reducing "hallway calls" for help, in which technicians passing through the office would be stopped by employees needing maintenance help.

Geographic assignment of maintenance techs addresses wide dispersion of facilities

The manager noted that the city's buildings are spread across a wide area. (The city covers 102 square miles.) To ensure that technicians are able to respond to maintenance concerns in a timely manner, two-person teams are assigned to a group of buildings usually clustered within a two-mile radius. (One exception is the team responsible for buildings in the northern part of the city; its cluster includes buildings within a radius of almost four miles.)

Aggressive preventive maintenance program minimizes occurrence of major problems

The city also operates an aggressive preventive maintenance program, with different preventive maintenance activities being conducted in each building every month. This allows maintenance staff to get to know their buildings well and spot minor problems before they become major ones, which saves the city time and money.

The city also assigns a nonmaintenance staff member as "building captain" in each city building. The building captain serves as a liaison between fellow building residents and the maintenance division. The captains are known to their fellow building residents and can be approached with concerns about maintenance, which they forward to maintenance staff. In addition, all employees are welcome and able to contact the maintenance division directly if they prefer.

Case Profile

Population:
206,735

Square miles:
102

Median household income:
$42,214

Form of government:
Council-manager

For additional information about the practices described in this case study, please contact Scott Jones, maintenance and operations manager, at jonessc@ci.reno.nv.us.

Maintenance staff also try to make personal contact with the building captains each week while they are carrying out preventive maintenance or repairs; these contacts help them determine whether there are any other maintenance concerns that need to be addressed.

Real-time, online service request system speeds responses

The city also employs a real-time, online service request system for its larger buildings, and within this system any city employee in one of these buildings can use an office computer to request maintenance help. This system has not only boosted the convenience for these employees, who no longer have to wait on the phone to request maintenance assistance; it has also improved maintenance staff efficiency by reducing "hallway calls" for help, in which technicians passing through the office would be stopped by employees needing maintenance help.

County of Yuma, AZ

Performance Indicator

- **Overall customer satisfaction with custodial service**

For FY 2006, Yuma County reported that 84 percent of customers rated custodial service as excellent or good. The mean and median proportions of excellent and good ratings for all jurisdictions reporting were 69 percent and 68 percent, respectively.

When asked how the county was able to achieve these performance levels, staff cited the following factors:

- **Open and frequent communication with custodial staff regarding individual and departmental performance**—Much of this communication takes place informally as supervisors visit job sites throughout the week and provide feedback regarding the work of individual staff members. It also takes place in more formal settings like monthly meetings of the custodial staff and quarterly meetings of the full general services department where customer feedback gleaned from surveys and direct interactions is shared. Evidence of good performance is celebrated, and opportunities for improvement are identified.
- **Recognition for high-quality performance**—Yuma County encourages custodial service supervisors to reinforce good performance on the spot by verbally acknowledging well-executed tasks and positive customer feedback at the earliest opportunity. The county believes strongly in the value of personal recognition timed closely with the incident deserving recognition. Employees may also be recognized again at their monthly or quarterly staff meetings.
- **Supervisor presence in the field**—The county's general services department also stresses the importance of having supervisory staff present in the field with its custodians. The goal of having supervisors in the field is to interact with customers, collecting and responding to their feedback, and to ensure that work is being well-executed by staff. When custodial staff members are absent, supervisors may also assist with execution of custodial work, further ensuring that custodial services are well provided.

Sharing customer feedback frequently

Yuma County has established a goal of having at least 85 percent of customers rate its custodial services as excellent or good. Supervisors report progress against this goal to custodial staff at their monthly meetings and at the quarterly meetings of the entire general services department. The general services department also reports progress toward this goal quarterly and annually to the county administrator.

Case Profile

Population:
1,260,950

Square miles:
385

Median household income:
$36,403

Form of government:
Council-manager

For additional information about the practices described in this case study, please contact Robert Lawson, general services director, at 928/817-5100 or robert.lawson@co.yuma.az.us.

Fire and EMS

Fire and EMS

City of Albany, OR

Performance Indicators

- **Customer satisfaction among those having contact with the fire department within the past 12 months**
- **Customer satisfaction among those having contact with the emergency medical services (EMS) within the past 12 months**

For FY 2006, the city of Albany reported that among customers having contact with the fire department, 97 percent rated the quality of contact as excellent. The mean and median values for all jurisdictions reporting were 71 percent and 78 percent, respectively.

That same year, among customers having contact with the EMS service, 96 percent rated the quality of contact as excellent. The mean and median values for all jurisdictions reporting were 82 percent and 89 percent, respectively.

Employees provide fire suppression, medical aid–and other assistance

When asked how the city achieved such high satisfaction ratings for its fire and EMS services, Albany's fire chief attributed much of this success to employees' drive to meet not only customers' direct emergency fire and medical service needs, but also other needs that become apparent while they are responding to a call. The chief noted that all fire and EMS staff are empowered and encouraged to assist customers directly or by referral in meeting needs for food, shelter, home repair, and other services. Moreover, employees have responded by doing such things as purchasing and delivering groceries to a needy family, performing yard work for an ill resident, replacing doors and windows damaged while gaining emergency access to residences, arranging and funding hotel accommodations for fire victims, and much more.

Staff state that customer service is not simply talked about at the Albany Fire Department; it is embedded in the culture.

City staff noted that Albany's emergency call volume makes the city one of the busiest fire departments in the state of Oregon (on a per capita basis), yet department employees continue to strive to meet customer needs well beyond those normally associated with an emergency response. Staff state that customer service is not simply talked about at the Albany Fire Department, it is embedded in the culture.

Community outreach is essential

Albany officials explained that the department also has an active community outreach program, which enables staff to interact—and build relationships—with citizens in settings beyond direct service provision, further promoting positive customer impressions.

- **Safety equipment provision**—Through its Community Assistance Fund and other public outreach programs, the fire department distributes

Case Profile

Population:
46,610

Square miles:
18

Median household income:
$39,409

Form of government:
Council-manager

For additional information about the practices described in this case study, please contact Kevin Kreitman, fire chief, at 541/917-7701 or kevin.kreitman@cityofalbany.net.

safety equipment like bike helmets, smoke detectors, carbon monoxide detectors, home escape ladders, residential key boxes, and grab bars for seniors and disabled residents—all free of charge. One very popular program allows residents to borrow water safety vests. Being home to a public pool, water park, and multiple waterways, water safety is a priority in the city. Since the vest loan program was introduced in 2006, there have been no drowning deaths in the district.

The department also provides residential sprinkler systems in Habitat for Humanity homes (in cooperation with fire sprinkler contractors), taxi rides when an ambulance is unwarranted, and college scholarships.

- **Emotional support**—Albany's fire department has a chaplain who provides services to department members and members of the public. The chaplain also responds on emergency calls, providing comfort and assistance to victims and their families.
- **Neighborhood activities**—The department also hosts an annual treasure hunt when residents are invited into their local firehouses for family activities like fire engine rides, equipment demonstrations, and other family-friendly fire safety activities. The event helps to show firefighters and EMS personnel as neighbors and friends and promotes the development of positive relationships between department staff and residents.
- **Safety instruction**—The department also offers fire and personal safety classes to schools, child care centers, recreation centers, and other programs serving children and senior citizens, including two four-day summer day camps for children entering the fourth, fifth, and sixth grades. During the camps, children are able to interact with firefighters and police officers informally and participate in various safety programs and activities in a fun, interactive environment.

Customer service training enhances outreach

In addition to its outreach efforts, the department requires in-depth customer service training for firefighters and EMS personnel to ensure that they provide the most compassionate care possible. The training begins with new employees. At the academy, all employees are taught that excellent customer service is required of all employees—and that it is important "not to disqualify the customer with our qualifications," in other words, to speak and interact with customers in a manner that makes customers comfortable and that they can understand.

The department also provides several hours of refresher training in customer service each year. This training covers several topics:

- How to comfort trauma victims
- How to manage bystanders
- What customers are saying on their customer service surveys
- "Stations and equipment belong to the community"
- "Every citizen is a customer and shareholder regardless of their social or economic status."

City publicizes performance data

Albany publishes a quarterly performance report that includes these and other measures. It is available on the Internet and is shared directly with the city council and other local government officials.

Another report, regarding the Albany Fire Fighters Community Assistance Fund (AFFCAF) and its activities, is also distributed by e-mail every two months. This report is shared with all fire department employees and the city manager.

City of Austin, TX

Case Profile

Population:
707,952

Square miles:
251

Median household income:
$43,731

Form of government:
Council-manager

Performance Indicator

- **Civilian (non-employee) fire deaths per 100,000 population**

For FY 2006, the city of Austin reported 1.13 civilian (non-employee) fire deaths per 100,000 population. The mean and median values for all jurisdictions reporting that year were 0.92 and 0.00 respectively. As it compared its data with data of other ICMA Center for Performance Measurement™ (CPM) jurisdictions in FY 2006 and other years, the city of Austin recognized that its performance could be improved and it conducted further research to develop improvement strategies.

City uses CPM data to analyze rise in fire deaths

For many years, the city of Austin experienced an average of five to six accidental fire deaths per year. In FY 2002 and FY 2003, however, both the number of fatalities and the fire death rate per 100,000 residents nearly doubled, and Austin scored among the highest in death rates in comparison with similar cities. In response, the fire department intensively studied local fire deaths and determined that the core problem was inadequate maintenance of smoke alarms.

Poor smoke alarm maintenance was the culprit

The result was the development of a massive public education program, geared to the general public, to encourage the routine testing and maintenance of smoke alarms. After the deaths of three young boys in a Christmas Eve fire, a local marketing firm volunteered time and materials to develop "Freddy the Finger," a cartoon mascot that urged residents to "put a finger on it" and test their smoke alarms. The general public was targeted because the data at that time indicated the risk of having a nonworking smoke alarm occurred among many disparate population subgroups.

Education campaign helped reduce fire deaths—for a time

After the Freddy the Finger campaign was launched in July 2003, for two years in a row fire deaths dropped to historic lows for Austin. Only one fire death each occurred in FY 2004 and FY 2005, yielding a fire death rate among the lowest in comparison with other CPM communities. During that time, Freddy the Finger was also credited with six "saves," incidents when residents called the fire department to report that smoke alarms they had recently fixed in response to the campaign had subsequently alerted them to fires in their homes.

But recently fire deaths in Austin have surged again (see the graph on the next page). Eight fire deaths occurred in both FY 2006 and FY 2007, yielding a death rate that, while similar to comparison cities, is still unacceptably high for Austin. Analysis of the most recent deaths has yielded a new insight: an emphasis on testing smoke alarms, while appropriate for the general public, is not an effective approach for the elderly, a population segment that experiences both a high risk of fire death and barriers to effectively maintaining battery-operated smoke alarms in their homes.

For additional information regarding the practices described in this case study, please contact Shannon Szymczak, acting corporate budget manager, at Shannon.Szymczak@ci.austin.tx.us.

Further analysis indicated that targeted assistance for the elderly is necessary

Statistics show that, similar to the elderly nationally, the elderly in Austin are significantly more likely to die in fires than other population subgroups. In the 2000 census, only 9 percent of the city's residents were over 60 years of age, yet that age group accounted for 38 percent of Austin fire fatalities between 2000 and 2007 (see the graph below).

Why is fire so deadly for the elderly? Older homes, older smoke alarms—and perhaps slower or less able physical responses to fire danger—contribute to increased risk. According to the 2000 census, 92 percent of older heads of households live in single-family residences, which unlike apartments are not subject to routine fire inspections. Nearly three-fourths (71

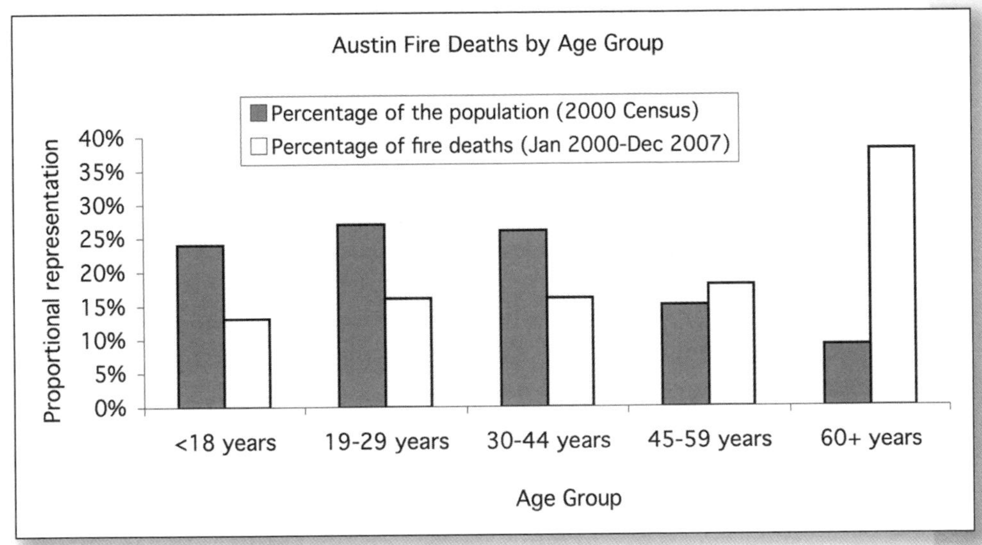

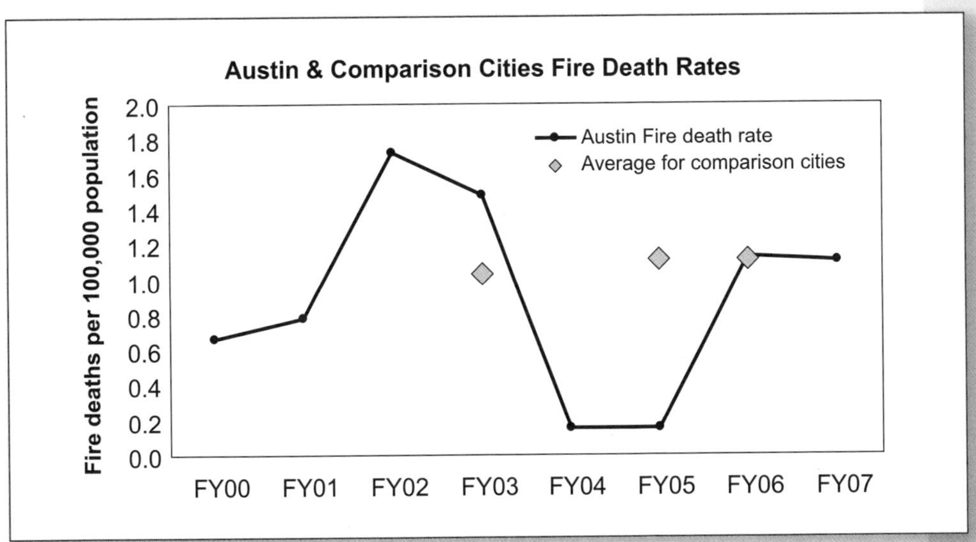

percent) live in housing built before 1980, a much higher percentage than found in the general population (52 percent). Houses built before 1980 are likely, if they have smoke alarms at all, to rely on smoke alarms powered by batteries instead of hard-wired into the electrical system. Older smoke alarms also have failure rates that increase by 3 percent each year; a smoke alarm that is 10 years old has only a 70 percent chance of working properly.

Citizen survey data provide additional insight

The city's annual customer survey provided further, more direct information on the fire risks of older homeowners. The fire department had added two questions about smoke alarms to the city budget office's annual survey of Austin residents. In the 2006 survey, older respondents were more likely than other residents to report not having a smoke alarm. Among those 65 years or older, 8.4 percent reported having no smoke alarm, compared with 6.5 percent for the 55–64 age group and 4.8 percent among respondents less than 55 years old. The differences among age groups were statistically significant.

Nearly one-fifth (19 percent) of those with smoke alarms who were over age 65 were unable to report when they last changed smoke alarm batteries. Overall, only 70 percent of older respondents to the 2006 survey reported that they both had smoke alarms and changed batteries at least once a year.

Even when older persons remember to change batteries, the process of doing so creates an additional risk—the risk of falling while trying to reach alarms placed at or near ceiling height. According to the Centers for Disease Control, about one-third of the elderly experience falls in any given year. Falls are the leading cause of injury death for people age 65 and older, and they account for 95 percent of hip fractures.

Low-maintenance smoke alarms seem to be helping

Based on this analysis, the Austin Fire Department identified the need to provide the elderly with low-maintenance smoke alarms that are easy to test and do not require climbing ladders or chairs to replace batteries. The department obtained a grant from the Department of Homeland Security to purchase 2,500 low-maintenance smoke alarms with 10-year batteries; residents are able to test these alarms by remote control. The fire department has been aggressively marketing the program and building partnerships with groups that serve the elderly. Although it is still too soon to evaluate success, as of June 2008 there had been no accidental fire deaths in Austin (nearly three-quarters of the way through the FY 2008 fiscal year).

Performance measurement represents a key to reducing fire deaths in Austin

Performance measurement has contributed substantially to Austin's ability to identify trends in fire deaths and see how Austin's rates compare with data in other communities. Performance measurement data are especially well suited for identifying problems that need to be addressed.

One challenge, after problems have been identified, is to figure out their causes; this requires additional time, effort, and sometimes data resources. In addition to existing data systems and census data, the Austin Fire Department benefited substantially from having smoke alarm questions in the community survey. Although community surveys have been used primarily to obtain feedback about government services, one potential further use has been to adapt them to measure community risks to facilitate the planning of mitigation efforts.

City of Henderson, NV

Case Profile

Population:
257,838

Square miles:
98

Median household income:
$56,857

Form of government:
Council-manager

Performance Indicator

- **Customer satisfaction among those having contact with the emergency medical services (EMS) within the past 12 months**

For FY 2006, the city of Henderson reported that 95 percent of customers rated emergency medical services as excellent. The mean and median proportions of excellent ratings for all jurisdictions reporting were 82 percent and 89 percent, respectively.

The city attributes its high customer satisfaction ratings to its relentless pursuit of customer service excellence, which is evident in

- Customer service training
- Satisfaction surveys sent to every customer (with individual results sent to every employee)
- Careful study and application of results.

Intensive customer service training conducted by the fire chief

In Henderson, the fire chief personally conducts the customer service training required for all emergency medical staff, demonstrating unequivocally that customer service is a departmental priority. This training is presented to all new employees.

High touch follow-up with EMS customers

The city also emphasizes the importance of follow-up with all customers. Every EMS customer, whether transported or not, receives a customer service survey by mail with a prepaid return envelope. Response rates averaged 36 percent during FY 2006.

These customer service surveys are tailored by the type of service received by the patient. Separate surveys are available for

- Cardiac
- Orthopedic
- Respiratory
- Non-transport patients.

Results are tracked by patient type to ensure that customer service results are consistent across types.

Henderson staff also note that they send their customer satisfaction surveys separate from any billing information to

- Ensure that the survey itself is the focus of the mailing
- Minimize the influence of payment concerns on customer reports of service quality.

The fire chief personally contacts all customers who on their surveys request department follow-up.

In addition to these department-specific customer service surveys, Henderson also regularly conducts scientific surveys of all residents. In recent

For additional information about the practices described in this case study, please contact Steven Goble, division chief, Special Operations, at 702/267-2218 or steven.goble@cityofhenderson.com.

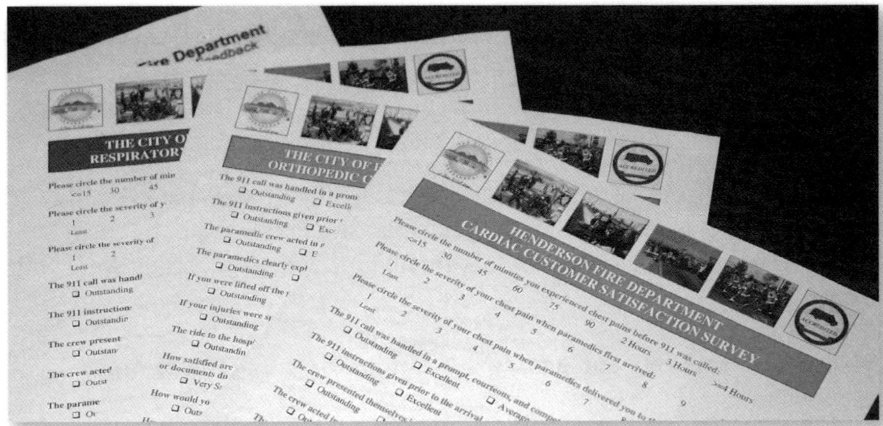

Henderson surveys its fire and EMS customers based on the types of services they receive.

years, the city has employed the National Citizen Survey™ service (offered by ICMA in partnership with the National Research Center in Boulder, Colorado) to conduct an annual mail survey. The city engages a local firm to conduct a telephone survey approximately once every three years.

Employees—and their supervisors—receive customer feedback monthly

Each month, EMS personnel receive personalized summaries of feedback received from the customers they served, frequently accompanied by copies of actual surveys with narrative feedback in respondents' own handwriting. This helps to emphasize the personal nature of EMS work—and the importance of treating every patient with dignity and respect.

Monthly feedback summaries are also shared with the fire chief, battalion chiefs, and the medical director.

Chief recognizes employees for achieving desired results

The chief personally contacts employees who achieve high customer service ratings to thank them for their good work. Supervisors may also recognize employees for exceptional customer service through the citywide staff recognition program.

Ongoing study and application of results

Henderson's emergency medical service has been emphasizing high-quality customer service since 1995 when department leaders launched their continuous improvement program with the question, "How do we prove—and build upon—our good reputation?"

Department staff began by researching best practices in data collection and analysis and used them to implement the department's customer survey in 1998. Staff continue today by revising the survey as necessary, periodically conducting special surveys (like a recent special survey of nontransport patients), and sharing their results with employees, appointed and elected leaders, accreditation agencies, and the public.

City of Highland Park, IL

Case Profile

Population:
31,365

Square miles:
13

Median household income:
$100,967

Form of government:
Council-manager

Performance Indicator

- **One- and two-family residential structure fires confined to room of origin**

For FY 2006, the city of Highland Park reported that it was able to confine 90 percent of one- and two-family residential structure fires to the room of origin. The mean and median values for all jurisdictions reporting were both 57 percent.

Well-placed stations and aggressive automatic aid promote rapid responses

When asked how the city has had such great success in confining fires to room of origin, Highland Park officials cited the city's rapid response system. They noted that the city responds to nearly 95 percent of fire calls in five minutes or less, and they attributed this to

- **Well-positioned fire stations**—The city boasts the presence of one fire station for every 4.2 square miles on average
- **An aggressive automatic aid program**—While many jurisdictions in the United States have mutual aid agreements with neighboring communities, in the Chicago area (where Highland Park is located), initial response automatic aid is aggressively employed to ensure that responders are always summoned from the closest fire station regardless of whether the station lies within the same legal jurisdiction as the subject of the call for assistance.

Other factors cited by the city as likely contributors to being able to confine fires to room of origin include:

- **Installing central station automatic alarm systems**—With all businesses and many homes having fire alarms connected to monitoring services (either private or city run), fires are detected quickly and the alarms are reported rapidly to the fire department, thus allowing for early suppression.
- **Adding sprinklers during home remodels**—The city recommends that sprinklers be added to the furnace room during all home remodeling projects. This recommendation is communicated to the property owner during the plan review and inspection process.
- **Enforcing building codes**—The city adheres to national building code standards—and enforces them aggressively—thus helping to prevent fires in the first place and discouraging the spread of fires that do occur.
- **Educating the public**—The city also sends firefighters into local schools to teach children about the importance of fire safety. The firefighters encourage children to remind their parents about replacing smoke detector batteries, eliminating extension cords, and implementing other fire safety measures.

For additional information about the practices described in this case study, please contact Patrick Brennan, deputy city manager, at 847/926-1003 or pbrennan@cityhpil.com.

Quarterly performance reporting maintains focus

In addition to measures explicitly intended to help confine fires to the room of origin, the Highland Park Fire Department also tracks performance on this measure and others to ensure that department personnel remain focused on performance.

The department reports its performance statistics to the city manager once each quarter and also compares its own performance with that of peer communities annually. Where differences are found between Highland Park and other communities, staff conduct research to determine the reasons for the differences and whether techniques in use in other communities might result in improvements in Highland Park.

County of Miami-Dade, FL

Case Profile

Population:
2,246,848

Square miles:
1964

Median household income:
$37,418

Form of government:
Council-administrator/manager

Performance Indicator

- **One- and two-family residential structure fires confined to room of origin**

For FY 2006, the county of Miami–Dade reported that of the number of one- and two- family residential structure fire incidents 84 percent were confined to the room of origin. The mean and median values for all jurisdictions reporting were both 57 percent.

Set dispatch goals

Miami–Dade County attributes much of its success in confining one- and two-family residential structure fires to the room of origin to its excellent dispatch times. The fire and rescue department works toward the goal of dispatching the full complement of units needed to respond to a structure fire (regardless of the structure's occupancy classification) within 80 seconds of receiving the call. (At the end of FY 2008, the county boasted an average time from receipt of call to dispatch of just 65 seconds.)

By regularly reviewing the number, type, and location of fire and rescue calls, the department has been able to discern shifting areas of peak demand and now regularly adjusts the placement of the fleet and fire apparatus to better respond to these shifting demands.

Establish clear and informed dispatch strategy

To ensure the quickest (and most effective) dispatching practices possible, Miami–Dade County developed its *Strategy for Alarm Assignments* in 1995. The strategy outlines, among other things, standards for dispatching the appropriate resources to fire, rescue, and other emergency incidents in a timely manner. The strategy has helped to streamline the handling of calls for service at the dispatch point and has promoted uniform responses by call type.

Use technology effectively

The implementation of a new computer-aided dispatch system in August 2005 also helped to minimize response time (and promote confinement of fires to room of origin). The new CAD system features an automated vehicle locator capability that has improved response times by allowing dispatch personnel to find and send the closest available unit to the scene of a fire (or other emergency), rather than having to notify the closest fire station and dispatch a parked unit from that location.

The county uses the off-the-shelf Motorola Premier CAD System, which was selected after much research and a long request for proposals process.

For additional information about the practices described in this case study, please contact Maria Reyes, division manager, at maria.reyes@miamidade.gov.

Analyze the data and manage your fleet accordingly

Miami–Dade County also promotes timely responses and fire confinement by monitoring performance on an ongoing basis:

- Twice each month, division fire chiefs meet to discuss fire events and look for and address emerging trends across the county.
- Once each month, county staff review the types and locations of the fire rescue calls, again seeking any trends that may require attention.
- Once each quarter, trends in the data are assessed again, and progress against goals in the county's balanced scorecard is reported. County departments, along with assistant county managers and staff from the Office of Strategic Business Management (OSBM), conduct quarterly business review meetings to assess trends in the data and progress against goals reported in the department's scorecards.
- Moreover, the fire department conducts monthly business review meetings and annual strategic planning workshops with executive staff, division chiefs and managers, and bureau chiefs and managers to revisit previously established departmental and division goals and outcomes.

One benefit of frequent examination of the county's fire data has been better management of the county's fire fleet—both vehicles and apparatus. By regularly reviewing the number, type, and location of fire and rescue calls, the department has been able to discern shifting areas of peak demand and now regularly adjusts the placement of the fleet and fire apparatus to better respond to these shifting demands.

Promote accountability through public reporting

The fire and rescue department—like all departments in the county—is also responsible for reporting its performance on a number of measures featured on the county's balanced scorecard. The department closely monitors its performance on scorecard measures and posts progress reports to the county's public Web site at the end of each quarter.

Within the fire and rescue department, each division maintains its own scorecard; these division scorecards help with internal monitoring and also keep the fire chief informed. A number of the key measures are included in the performance appraisals of assistant chiefs and directors and division chiefs and managers.

Since 2005, the county has used a Web-based software system called ActiveStrategy to collect and manage its performance information. The system links the county's strategic plan, operational objectives, and performance indicators. Departments enter their information into the system and see it linked to the county's organizationwide strategic objectives. Integration of the software into the regular work of the departments also encourages the culture change required to drive the operational results desired.

Fleet Management

Fleet Management

City of Chesapeake, VA

Performance Indicators

- **Customer satisfaction with the quality of fleet maintenance services**
- **Customer satisfaction with the timeliness of fleet maintenance services**

For FY 2006, the city of Chesapeake reported that 97.3 percent of customers rated the quality of fleet maintenance services as excellent or good. The mean and median values for all jurisdictions reporting that year were 89.7 percent and 86.2 percent, respectively.

The city also reported that 94.6 percent of customers rated the timeliness of fleet maintenance services as excellent or good. The mean and median were 88.6 percent and 81.8 percent respectively.

Fleet customer satisfaction has improved over time

When Chesapeake's current fleet manager joined the department in 2001, he recognized that there was widespread dissatisfaction among customers of the fleet maintenance department. He learned of these customer concerns from a recent audit and discussions with the deputy city manager and other staff.

The fleet manager sought to determine the causes of the dissatisfaction by meeting with department heads, assessing their needs, and discussing better ways to meet those needs.

In addition to seeking customer input, the fleet manager also asked employees how they thought the department could improve. He met one-on-one with each mechanic and also led staff in a group visioning process.

As a result of these discussions, the fleet manager implemented a training program for all staff that included customer service instruction and computer skills classes. The computer training focused on ensuring that work order information was entered correctly so that workload data could be tracked accurately. The data are now charted and posted in the department so that staff and customers alike can monitor performance and identify improvement targets.

The fleet manager also implemented a formal customer feedback system, requiring that all customers be provided with a satisfaction survey after completion of each maintenance request. The department also sponsors quarterly user group meetings where staff explain department policies and practices and seek customer feedback.

City saves customer and staff time with holistic approach to vehicle repair

The city sought to boost customer satisfaction further by implementing a holistic approach to repairing vehicles. When a vehicle was brought in for repair under the previous approach, the problem identified by the customer was addressed, and the vehicle was returned to the customer. Now, when a vehicle is brought in for repair, the customer-identified problem is addressed

Case Profile

Population:
220,068

Square miles:
353

Median household income:
$60,187

Form of government:
Council-manager

For additional information about the practices described in this case study, please contact George Hrichak, fleet manager, at 757/382-3375 or ghrichak@cityofchesapeake.net.

and a general diagnostic check of the entire vehicle is also performed—and any other problems that might be found are fixed.

This has helped the fleet maintenance staff manage its time—and customers' time—much more effectively. Individual visits for each vehicle take slightly longer, but the number of visits to the repair facility has dropped dramatically.

In FY 2003, the city reported completing approximately 1,240 repair orders per month and spending about 2.6 hours on each work order. By FY 2006, the time spent on each work order had risen to about 3.7 hours per work order, but the number of repair orders had dropped to approximately 860 per month.

Outsourcing parts department saved additional resources

The city was able to streamline operations further by outsourcing its parts department. (Employees in the parts department were offered positions elsewhere in the city.) The city sold its existing inventory, earning $115,000 in revenue over five years, and reduced its list of out-of-stock items from an average of 488 items per month in FY 2003 to an average of only 14 items per month in FY 2007.

Instituting lasting practices to keep costs controlled

Chesapeake's fleet maintenance operation also seeks to demonstrate respect for customers' time by providing dedicated preventive maintenance mechanics and convenient online scheduling for preventive maintenance work. Turnaround time for preventive maintenance appointments is generally just one hour. The fleet maintenance staff also helps customers remember to schedule their next preventive maintenance appointment by placing a commercial-style reminder sticker in the vehicle before it leaves the shop.

To make sure that customers comply with preventive maintenance requirements, the city also restricts fuel access when preventive maintenance is past due. With implementation of the reminder system and fuel restrictions, the city was able to reduce past due preventive maintenance work orders from 40 per month in FY 2002 to only 17 per month by FY 2006. (Past due preventive maintenance work orders dropped further in FY 2007 to an average of only four per month.)

City of Oklahoma City, OK

Performance Indicators

- **Customer satisfaction with the quality of fleet maintenance services**
- **Customer satisfaction with the timeliness of fleet maintenance services**

For FY 2006, the city of Oklahoma City's fleet maintenance department reported that 94.6 percent of its customers rated the quality of fleet maintenance services as excellent or good. The mean and median values for all jurisdictions reporting were 89.7 percent and 86.2 percent, respectively.

With regard to the timeliness of maintenance, 93.2 percent of Oklahoma City's customers gave a rating of excellent or good. The mean value was 88.6 percent, and the median value was 81.8 percent.

Focus on the customer

The city of Oklahoma City attributes its high customer satisfaction rating to several factors:

- **Strong customer orientation, backed up by training**—To promote positive customer relations, Oklahoma City provides customer service training for its fleet maintenance staff. The city emphasizes that customers' first impressions—whether interacting with the shop manager, a service writer, or a technician—influence their overall opinion of the operation. Thus, all employees are encouraged and trained to treat customers well.
- **ASE-certified technicians**—To ensure that maintenance work is performed well—which promotes "up time" for vehicles and in turn boosts customer satisfaction—the city encourages all technicians to gain certification from the National Institute for Automotive Service Excellence (ASE), the industry's certification leader.
- **Focus on up time**—The city also frames its efforts to keep vehicles in service as "boosting up time" rather than "minimizing down time." The city's current goal is to ensure up time of 95 percent or better for all vehicles.
- **Convenient scheduling options**—Oklahoma City also places great emphasis on customer convenience when providing preventive maintenance and other vehicle services. City staff may schedule vehicle inspections and preventive maintenance work with a dedicated mechanic at a time convenient for themselves. The work is then completed on the city's quick line while staff wait, if they desire.
- **Online service request tracking**—Customers who choose not to wait—because of a lengthy repair or other reason—can monitor the status of their service requests through the city's online tracking system. Fleet maintenance staff also use e-mail to update customers about changes in predicted completion times—after discovery of additional repair needs, for example—that may come up while they are working on a vehicle.

Case Profile

Population:
543,800

Square miles:
621

Median household income:
$37,375

Form of government:
Council-manager

For additional information about the practices described in this case study, please contact Patrick Morris, operations manager, at patrick.morris@okc.gov.

Customers have expressed great satisfaction with these information services.

Monitor results

To ensure that these customer satisfaction efforts are generating the desired results, the city also provides a point-of-service survey to each customer upon completion of every service request.

The shop manager also analyzes shop performance data each day to ensure that up time goals and other priorities are being met. The manager reviews the status of open work orders, examines new orders, and compares recent patterns for predicted versus actual service request completion times. With this information, the manager then sets the priorities for the day and assigns resources accordingly—all of which contribute to good productivity, which in turn promotes customer satisfaction.

Recognize good performance

Oklahoma City also seeks to promote employee satisfaction by recognizing top performers. Management staff examine productivity statistics each pay period, and they identify top-performing employees at regular staff meetings. Top performers for the quarter receive a paid day off and have their names placed on plaques displayed in the fleet maintenance shop and at the division headquarters.

City of Reno, NV

Performance Indicators

- **Customer satisfaction with the quality of fleet maintenance services**
- **Customer satisfaction with the timeliness of fleet maintenance services**

For FY 2006, the city of Reno's fleet maintenance division reported that 97.7 percent of its customers rated the quality of service as excellent or good. The mean and median values for all jurisdictions reporting were 89.7 percent and 86.2 percent, respectively.

With regard to the timeliness of service, 97.7 percent of Reno's fleet customers gave a rating of excellent or good. The mean value was 88.6 percent, and the median value was 81.8 percent.

Fix it right the first time, schedule well

When asked how the city's fleet maintenance operation achieved such high satisfaction ratings, the manager cited two factors:

1. Fixing problems correctly on the first try
2. Scheduling work properly.

Certified techs promote proper diagnosis and repair

To ensure that problems are diagnosed accurately and repaired properly during a vehicle's first visit to the garage, Reno's fleet manager has strongly encouraged all mechanics to become certified by the National Institute for Automotive Service Excellence (ASE). The fleet manager pointed out that ASE certification ensures third-party, industry-accepted assessment and recognition of a mechanic's education and skill—and that pursuit of certification (which requires a great deal of study) demonstrates a mechanic's own commitment to professional excellence.

Fix-it-right-the-first-time philosophy saves $20,000

Beginning in 2003, as the city's fleet manager was beginning to address what he considered to be a higher-than-desired comeback rate that at the time was approximately 2.0 percent, he decided to encourage certification. (The comeback rate refers to the frequency with which vehicles are returned to the shop for the same repair problem.)

That same year, three of Reno's eight mechanics were ASE certified. By 2008, seven had earned ASE certification, and the comeback rate had dropped to less than 0.5 percent. That may not appear dramatic at first, but it translates to a cash savings of approximately $20,000 per year.

The city also boasts of having its parts technicians and counter staff ASE certified, further enhancing the fleet maintenance staff's ability to diagnose and repair problems correctly during a vehicle's first visit.

To encourage certification, the city reimburses its staff for all successfully completed ASE tests and pays a modest bonus to certified employees. This bonus is paid each pay period as long as the technician remains certified.

Case Profile

Population:
206,735

Square miles:
102

Median household income:
$42,214

Form of government:
Council-manager

For additional information about the practices described in this case study, please contact Bruce Mullin, fleet manager, at mullinb@ci.reno.nv.us.

Scheduling all routine work saves time

Reno believes that ASE certification may also promote more efficient repairs by its mechanics, which in turn may boost timeliness, but the fleet manager points to the city's fleet maintenance scheduling system as the most significant factor in its high ratings for timeliness.

Reno's fleet manager schedules all nonemergency maintenance on city vehicles. A computer program is used to track the need for oil changes, tire rotation, and other standard maintenance for each vehicle, and an electronic alert is issued whenever such work is needed.

Communicate, communicate, communicate

The fleet department has established in each city department a fleet department liaison to whom the department sends a monthly e-mail notice that lists all vehicles in the department for which maintenance is due. The list also notes any vehicles for which regular maintenance is past due. Fleet staff then work with the liaisons to schedule work on the vehicles. In cases of a vehicle that is used by a single employee, the liaison may ask that employee to contact the fleet department directly to schedule the work.

Liaisons and individual employees are welcome to specify repair times that are most convenient for themselves. For some departments, loaner vehicles are available for use while maintenance is performed on their regular vehicles. Runners are also available to ferry staff back and forth to their offices to facilitate drop-off and pickup of their vehicles in cases when loaner vehicles are not available. For some high-intensity users like police officers, fleet department staff also provide direct pickup and drop-off of the vehicles.

No waiting for scheduled work

For regular maintenance, mechanics are scheduled to be ready and waiting to perform the work as soon as the vehicle is dropped off, thus reducing wait time for return of the vehicle. If a repair problem is found during the course of regular maintenance, customers are immediately notified of the problem and of the estimated time to correct it. (The fleet maintenance director cited this communication as another factor contributing to high satisfaction with service quality.)

Floater accommodates unexpected jobs

A "floating mechanic" is usually available to accommodate unexpected repair work without compromising the timeliness of other scheduled work.

Highways & Road Maintenance

Highways & Road Maintenance

Town of Fishers, IN

Performance Indicator

- **Citizen satisfaction with snow removal**

For FY 2006, the town of Fishers reported that 55 percent of citizens rated the quality of snow removal efforts as excellent or good. The mean and median values for all jurisdictions reporting that year were 56 percent and 54 percent, respectively. (These data were collected using the National Citizen Survey™, available through the ICMA Center for Performance Measurement™ [CPM].)

Town officials were not satisfied with this result; they wanted to do better.

Prior to administration of the survey, Fishers removed snow primarily with a workforce made up of town employees, who cleared arterial streets first and then neighborhood streets. The town sought additional help from contractors when accumulations exceeded 14 inches.

Consider all options for boosting performance

To improve snow removal operations and boost citizen satisfaction, the town adjusted its plan for the next snow season. It chose to augment town forces with contract help for every storm (not just those with large accumulations).

The town also conducted an inventory of its streets to ensure that town snow removal resources were dedicated to clearing public streets. Research indicated that in some prior snow emergencies, the town had mistakenly removed snow from private streets (those managed by homeowner associations, for example) before it finished work on public streets.

Make a choice that balances performance and cost

The town found that using contract assistance for every snowstorm was expensive, and it is now developing criteria for determining when to use contract assistance. These criteria are expected to balance the need to remove snow quickly with the need to remove it cost-effectively.

Fishers is also investigating other ways to improve its snow removal program:

- **Traffic signal overrides for snowplows**—To help snowplow drivers manage rush-hour snow removal requirements better, the town is equipping its snowplows with the Opticom traffic signal override system that many ambulances and other public safety vehicles have. Major problems with snowplow movements in traffic during a rush-hour snow storm in February 2007 pointed out the need for this system.
- **Chemical treatments**—Fishers also continues to examine salt and other treatments available to improve road conditions in snowy and icy weather.

Anecdotal evidence suggests that Fishers's efforts have boosted customer satisfaction with the town's snow removal efforts. The town plans to conduct another survey to verify these impressions in 2008 or 2009.

Case Profile

Population:
62,725

Square miles:
29

Median household income:
$75,638

Form of government:
Council-manager

For additional information about the practices described in this case study, please contact Jeffrey Heiking, director of engineering and public works, at 317/595-3162 or heikingj@fishers.in.us.

County of Lyon, NV

Case Profile

Population:
48,860

Square miles:
2,431

Median household income:
$43,324

Form of government:
Council-administrator/manager

Performance Indicator

- **Paved lane miles assessed in satisfactory condition or better as a percentage of total paved lane miles**

For FY 2006, Lyon County reported that 98.6 percent of its roads were rated in satisfactory or better condition. The mean and median values for all jurisdictions reporting were 79.4 percent and 83.2 percent, respectively.

When asked how the county was able to keep such a high proportion of its roads in good condition, county staff noted two factors:

- A scheduled road maintenance program
- Adoption of a new road-sealing product.

In accordance with the maintenance program, the county's road division director stated that the county works to slurry-seal or chip-seal all roads at least once every five years. He also noted that the county hires a large contingent of temporary workers each summer to perform permanent repairs to road problems that may have received temporary fixes earlier in the year, further promoting good road condition.

Polymer-modified sealant promotes better road condition

Since 2005, the county has been sealing most of its roads with a relatively new polymer-modified pavement sealant product. Lyon County's road division director noted that he has observed the product's unusual ability to appear to heal cracks in road surfaces rather than simply fill them. This healing property can lengthen the life of a road beyond that which simple crack sealing does, which ensures good road condition and may even save money that would otherwise be needed to repave at shorter intervals.

Although the product has been used for only a few years, Lyon County staff anticipate that the polymer-modified sealant will preserve good road condition longer than products that were used previously and perhaps will extend the life of the county's roads overall.

Polymer-modified sealant performs well in many conditions

The product was also chosen because it performs well in a variety of weather conditions. Lyon County is located in the high desert of northwestern Nevada and experiences changing weather throughout the year, with snow in winter and warm, dry conditions in summer. The polymer-modified sealant has been shown to perform well in such changing conditions.

The county also noted that in FY 2006 many miles of new roads constructed as part of new housing subdivisions were brought under county control, thereby boosting the proportion of new roads in the county's inventory.

For additional information about the practices described in this case study, please contact Gary Fried, road division director, at 775/577-5011 or gfried@lyon-county.org.

City of Phoenix, AZ

Performance Indicators

- **Road rehabilitation expenditures per paved lane mile**
- **Paved lane miles assessed in satisfactory condition or better as a percentage of total paved lane miles assessed**

For FY 2006, the city of Phoenix reported spending $1,545 per paved lane mile for road rehabilitation. The mean and median values for all jurisdictions reporting were $3,193 and $2,597, respectively.

That same year, the city also reported that 91 percent of paved lane miles assessed received a rating of satisfactory or better. The mean and median values were 79 percent and 83 percent, respectively.

Good weather helps

When asked how the city of Phoenix achieves such good results with regard to road rehabilitation expenditures and road condition ratings, staff noted that Phoenix's warm climate is an important factor. Without the ravages of snow, ice, and other freezing conditions, Phoenix's roads generally require fewer repairs than roads in localities that experience colder weather.

Even compared with other Sunbelt communities, however, Phoenix's performance stands out.

Two other factors to which staff attribute the city's success in providing smooth roads at below-average cost are:

- Use of rubberized asphalt
- Stable staffing.

Stable, non-expansive foundation soils also contribute to pavement longevity in the city.

City staff invented—and apply—rubberized asphalt

In the late 1980s, engineers at the city of Phoenix began seeking a road resurfacing material that would both improve long-term "rideability" and generally extend the life of the city's streets. They tried "hot in place" repairs, overlay fabric, and other techniques, but they settled on the use of an in-house invention known as rubberized asphalt.

Rubberized asphalt is created by mixing 20 percent vulcanized rubber (from old tires) with 80 percent asphalt. When it is compared with other road surface materials, it boasts a number of desirable properties:

- Less cracking
- Self-healing of many (although not all) cracks that do occur
- Less warping
- Less road noise.

Rubberized asphalt roads last 20 years and longer without an overlay

Staff also determined that, although the up-front cost of rubberized asphalt is approximately twice that of traditional asphalt, the life of the material is

Case Profile

Population:
1,507,130

Square miles:
516

Median household income:
$42,353

Form of government:
Council-manager

For additional information about the practices described in this case study, please contact Brian Hinrichs, street maintenance superintendent, at brian.hinrichs@phoenix.gov.

more than twice that of traditional asphalt. Roads surfaced with the material in the late 1980s had yet to require new overlays as of 2008. Moreover, the rubberized asphalt roads require fewer crack seals and other ongoing maintenance than traditional asphalt and pavement roads owing to the self-healing properties of the material.

Staff stability promotes innovation

City staff also note that the stability of Phoenix's engineering staff promotes innovations like invention and testing of rubberized asphalt—which is now commercially available and used on roads throughout the southwestern United States.

Members of the city's senior engineering team have an average tenure of 25.5 years. Because staff members have worked at the city for many years, they have had the opportunity to suggest new approaches, test them, and implement those that work well.

Staff also note that data regarding road condition and staffing are monitored within the department throughout the year and reported in the city manager's annual report to the city council. The city evaluates pavement condition using the International Roughness Index, which is an industry standard index used by such organizations as the U.S. Department of Transportation and World Bank.

Housing

Housing

City of Colorado Springs, CO

Performance Indicator

- **Number of new low-moderate income housing units completed per $100,000 of public financial assistance**

For FY 2006, the city of Colorado Springs reported the number of new low-moderate income housing units completed per $100,000 of public financial assistance as 13.0. The mean and median for all jurisdictions reporting were 5.1 and 2.6, respectively.

Work with many funders and housing service providers to manage market fluctuations

To promote the construction and acquisition of new low-moderate income housing units (as well as the development of other mechanisms for providing low-moderate income housing), the city of Colorado Springs actively seeks funding from a wide variety of sources and partners with an array of housing service organizations. This two-pronged approach of working with multiple funding sources and provider organizations allows the city to adapt and respond to changes in the housing market.

The city of Colorado Springs does not own or manage housing units itself. Instead, it works primarily as a funding conduit, helping local housing service organizations develop new low-moderate income housing units. The city also provides rental assistance directly to some families.

Among the types of housing development assistance the city offers are

- Grants
- Loans
- Expedited application review
- Fee waivers (for development plan review fees and some engineering review fees for affordable housing projects)
- Fee deferrals (of up to 10 years for water and wastewater development fees for energy-efficient affordable housing projects; offered in partnership with the city's water department).

The fee waiver and fee deferral programs received recognition from the U.S. Department of Housing and Urban Development for innovative programming.

Build relationships and communicate

The city also encourages the development of new low-moderate income housing units by cultivating strong relationships with housing service organizations—both local and otherwise. The city's housing department shares information about available funding with partner organizations and encourages those partners to present ideas for applying the funding.

An example of a mutually beneficial relationship with a housing service provider is the city's relationship with the local Habitat for Humanity affiliate. With the city's help in securing home site funding, Habitat has been

Case Profile

Population:
394,914

Square miles:
194

Median household income:
$47,854

Form of government:
Council-manager

For additional information about the practices described in this case study, please contact: Chad Wright, affordable housing program manager, at cwright@springsgov.com.

able to capitalize on its expertise in the construction and funding of the homes themselves. The city considers this partnership to be a winner for both itself and Habitat because city residents gain homes and Habitat fulfills its mission.

The city also strives to maintain open communication with its partners, which further promotes development of new units. City staff meet regularly with housing partners to discuss what the partners are hearing and seeing "on the ground" in the housing development community and to exchange information about networking and funding opportunities.

Innovative partnership with local county government has further boosted low-moderate income housing development

One particularly innovative program that is helping to encourage the development of new low-moderate income housing units in Colorado Springs is the city's partnership with El Paso County. In 2003, the city and the county entered into a formal agreement to combine their private activity bond (PAB) capacity for affordable housing, which has provided a tremendous boost in both entities' ability to support multifamily housing development and mortgage assistance projects. (Through the partnership, mortgages worth approximately $135,000,000 were originated from 2003 to 2007; 61 percent of the borrowers were low-moderate income.)

The collaboration also allowed the city and county to boost their ability to secure additional PAB capacity through a statewide competition, thereby increasing the resources available to finance additional low-moderate income housing projects.

Track performance

The city of Colorado Springs tracks the performance of its housing department and community housing partners closely. The city works with partner organizations to develop program goals and communicate about progress toward those goals. The city and its partners also may adjust goals periodically in response to changes in the housing market. Some goals correspond to formal requirements from HUD, and others correspond to local housing development priorities.

The housing department in Colorado Springs analyzes performance data quarterly to track what is going on in the market; a strong relationship with the city's association of realtors proved to be very helpful to the city in these efforts.

Twice a year, the housing department appears before the city council. At its first presentation each year, the housing department explains to the council the goals it has set. At its second presentation in the middle of the year, the department reports on its progress in meeting the goals and describes any factors that may have influenced goal resetting. Department leaders stand accountable for meeting the goals established, but the city considers external factors such as market conditions and funding changes when judging results.

City of Salem, OR

Performance Indicators

- **Number of new low-moderate income housing units completed per $100,00 of public financial assistance for new housing**
- **Number of new low-moderate income housing units completed as a percentage of units needed**

For FY 2006, the city of Salem reported completing 25.3 new low-moderate income housing units per $100,000 of public financial assistance. The mean and median values for all jurisdictions reporting were 5.1 and 2.6, respectively.

The city also reported that it was able to complete 106 percent of the new low-moderate income housing units needed that year. The mean and median completion rates were 44.3 percent and 2.4 percent, respectively.

When asked how the city was able to complete so many new low-moderate income units that year—and so cost-efficiently—Salem staff noted several factors:

- **Conversion of existing units**—The city was able to bring approximately 485 existing housing units into the low-moderate income housing stock that year. The city partnered with residents, the local housing authority, and nonprofit developers to convert a number of different types of units into low-moderate income housing.
- **Marketing to developers**—The city aggressively markets the availability of housing development funds to potential developers, which in turn boosts the number of units completed.
- **Affordable housing market citywide**—The city enjoys relatively low-cost housing options throughout the jurisdiction; thus, there are perhaps more easily accessible options for low-moderate income housing than in other communities, and the available options can be brought into the low-moderate income housing stock relatively inexpensively.
- **Tax credits**—The availability of tax credits from the state and federal governments enabled the city to encourage the development of some new low-moderate income housing units that year, also.

Case Profile

Population:
147,250

Square miles:
47

Median household income:
$54,200

Form of government:
Council-manager

For more information about the practices described in this case study, please contact Rena B. Peck, federal programs manager, at 503/588-6162 or rpeck@cityofsalem.net.

County of Santa Barbara, CA

Case Profile

Population:
421,625

Square miles:
2,744

Median income:
$55,970

Form of government:
Council-administrator/manager

Performance indicator

- **Number of new low-moderate income housing units completed as a percentage of housing units needed**

For FY 2006, the county of Santa Barbara reported completing 116.8 percent of low- moderate income housing units needed. The mean and median values for all jurisdictions reporting were 44.3 percent and 2.4 percent, respectively.

The county needed 107 units, and 125 units were completed. For the FY 2004 reporting period (the next most recent year for which data are available), Santa Barbara County reported a need for 92 units, and it completed 34 (37.0 percent).

Plan strategically to meet projected need

County staff attribute some of their good performance to the fact that project completion rates vary from year to year. Projects are begun in one year and may take two, three, or more years to complete. Thus, many projects can be in progress in one year with few completed, and the next year many might be completed.

Also, it generally takes several years to accumulate the funding required to finance a housing project fully. Thus, efforts are considered from a long-term perspective. In FY 2006, one such project was a rental-housing development that had been in the pipeline for several years. Forty-three units in the rental-housing development were part of an inclusionary housing agreement with a local developer (setting aside 20 percent of the new units for affordable housing). Another rental-housing project with 229 units was completed in May 2008.

County staff predict that their FY 2006 performance will not be sustained in subsequent years because housing development costs continue to grow and federal funding continues to decline.

To shorten the time between builds, county staff are working on several other initiatives to meet various housing needs in the area. An assistance program for new home buyers should be reflected in the county's FY 2007 activities. For FY 2008, the county approved a 10-year plan for addressing homelessness in a comprehensive manner.

Form partnerships with neighboring localities to boost resources

Because the county's population data do not qualify the county independently to receive an annual allocation of federal affordable housing funds through the federal government's HOME Investment Partnerships Program, the county has partnered with several incorporated cities in the county (Santa Maria, Carpentaria, Lompoc, Solvang, and Buellton) to form a HOME Consortium. The consortium allows members to pool their population numbers to qualify for funding from the federal HOME program for the acquisition, rehabilitation, or new construction of rental apartment complexes, home ownership units, and transitional facilities for special needs individuals and families.

For additional information about the practices described in this case study, please contact John Torell, director of housing and community development, at torell@co.santa-barbara.ca.us.

Placed in the unique position of being a largely rural jurisdiction and having a very high-cost housing market (one of the top 10 in the nation), Santa Barbara County tends to face opposition when trying to site higher-density, affordable housing projects in rural areas. The HOME program has allowed the county not only to receive an annual allocation of federal affordable housing funding but also to cooperate on the location of new housing projects (sometimes within those incorporated jurisdictions' boundaries) and to negotiate together with those cities when attempting to meet state housing goals.

Human Resources

Human Resources

City of Chesapeake, VA

Performance Indicator

- **Number of working days to complete an external recruitment with testing**

For FY 2006, the city of Chesapeake reported spending an average of 25 working days to complete an external recruitment with testing. For all jurisdictions reporting that year, the mean and median time spans were 50 working days and 40 working days, respectively.

During FY 2004, the city of Chesapeake identified the time required to complete an external recruitment as a target for improvement. At the time, the city took an average of 40 working days to complete such a recruitment.

After researching options for reducing cycle time on this indicator, the city chose to implement an online application system (see the application on the next page). Research indicated that the transition to an online application system would save the time of one full-time equivalent clerical staff person who had previously managed the city's paper-based application system.

The city hired an outside contractor to develop the online system. Features of the system include:

- 24-hour access to job listings and application process for prospective applicants through the city's Web site
- 24-hour access to completed applications for hiring authorities
- Custom applications for each job with pre-populated job requirement fields.

Because many members of the public use computers at the city's libraries—and apply for city jobs using those computers—the human resources department also trained library staff to assist library patrons in completing the city's online job application. The city also installed five computer terminals (one with handicapped access) at city hall to allow members of the public to apply for city jobs.

After implementing the online application system, Chesapeake's cycle time for external recruitments with testing dropped from 40 working days in FY 2004 to 25 working days in FY 2006. The department monitored its progress using the ICMA Center for Performance Measurement™ (CPM) cycle time measures.

Case Profile

Population:
220,068

Square miles:
353

Median household income:
$60,187

Form of government:
Council-manager

For additional information about the practices described in this case study please contact: Mary Bullock, human resources director, at 757/382-6580 or mbullock@cityofchesapeake.net.

Create General Application

Page 1 of 7

For security purposes, this system automatically logs you off when it senses no activity for 60 minutes. Please click one of the **Save...** buttons at the bottom of the screen every 60 minutes in order to avoid losing your data.

*Required information is denoted with an asterisk.

Personal Information

* First Name:
* Middle Name: Please enter "NMN" if you do not have a middle name.
* Last Name:
* Address:
* City:
* State (enter NA if a non U.S. address):
* Zip Code:
* Last Four Digits of Social Security Number
* Home Phone: *(format: xxx-xxx-xxxx)*

Work Phone: *(format: xxx-xxx-xxxx)*

May we contact you at work? ○ Yes ○ No ◉ No Response

Cell/Other Phone: *(format: xxx-xxx-xxxx)*

Email Address:

Additional Information

* Are you currently employed by the City of Chesapeake? ○ Yes ○ No ◉ No Response

If yes, please give dates of employment, position held, and the department:

* Have you ever been employed by the City of Chesapeake? ○ Yes ○ No ◉ No Response

If yes, please give dates of employment, position held, and the department (please

Chesapeake accepts online job applications at http://www.jobs.cityofchesapeake.net.

Town of Queen Creek, AZ

Performance Indicator

- **Working days for external recruitment with testing**

For 2006, the town of Queen Creek reported that an average of 30 working days was required to complete an external recruitment with testing. The mean and median values for all jurisdictions reporting were 50 days and 40 days, respectively.

Tests administered on interview date

When asked how the town was able to keep recruiting times so low, the human resources director cited the fact that the town administers any necessary tests on the same day as a candidate's interview. Some organizations test and interview candidates on separate days, which may lengthen the time required to complete a recruitment.

The human resources manager noted that differences in when tests are administered may reflect differences in how the tests are used. He stated that Queen Creek uses tests to confirm that candidates are suitable for a position, and the tests are administered after the candidates' applications have been screened. In contrast, some other organizations use tests as an initial step to screen out potential candidates.

Cross-trained human resources staff

Queen Creek's human resources staff recently switched from a specialist orientation to a generalist orientation. Previously, staff members specialized in recruiting, classification and compensation, or performance evaluations. Now, staff members are cross-trained in all functions and support specific departments, but they are able to assist any department if a department's regular point of contact is not available. Because the staff is relatively small, this change has made the department much more efficient.

A few other helpful factors

The human resources director also noted that the town does not recruit for public safety positions, which sometimes require more recruiting time than other types of positions. In addition, the town has a relatively small staff and a good location, which the human resources director suggested may promote good recruiting times also.

Recruiting data are monitored quarterly through reports to the town's coordinator of ICMA Center for Performance Measurement™ (CPM) efforts and annually through reports to the town manager.

Case Profile

Population:
22,477

Square miles:
26

Median household income:
$63,702

Form of government:
Council-manager

For additional information about the practices described in this case study, please contact Bruce Gardner, human resources director, at bruce.gardner@queencreek.org.

Information Technology

Information Technology

City of Mesa, AZ

Performance Indicator

- **Help desk calls resolved at the time of call**

For FY 2006, the city of Mesa's information technology department reported that it was able to resolve 76 percent of its help desk calls at the time of the call. The mean and median values for all other jurisdictions reporting were 43 percent and 38 percent, respectively.

Make call resolution an explicit goal

Staff members of Mesa's information technology department attributed a great deal of their success in resolving help desk calls at the time of the call to the fact that it is their explicit goal to do so. They noted that the focus of Mesa's help desk is call resolution rather than dispatch of technicians. Help desk associates are able to dispatch by telephone technicians to remedy problems beyond their capability, but help desk staff are trained and encouraged to resolve as many calls themselves as they are able.

Help desk staff are trained in a wide variety of desktop applications and hardware elements and have real-time network monitoring capabilities—all of which empower them to solve the vast majority of users' problems within minutes.

To ensure continuous improvements in help desk service, the department conducts an audit of every call that could not be resolved at the time of the call to determine how a similar call might be handled more quickly in the future.

For calls that must be transferred to a technician, the help desk associate who begins the call maintains responsibility until its final resolution. This promotes continuity for the customer, who can always contact the responsible associate for status updates, and instills a sense of ownership in the associate, who is able to see each call through to its conclusion.

Prevent isolation of help desk staff

Mesa's help desk manager observed that the solitary nature of help desk work can sometimes be isolating and lead some staff to feel as if they are not an integral, valued part of the city's information technology department. These feelings can lead further to poor job performance for some employees. To prevent such outcomes and to build a strong, motivated customer service team, Mesa's help desk manager employs a number of measures to help representatives make connections with each other and the customers they serve:

- **Including help desk staff in department planning initiatives**—Help desk staff participate in department project planning and rollout of new hardware and software applications, giving them the opportunity to

Case Profile

Population:
455,984

Square miles:
131

Median household income:
$44,861

Form of government:
Council-manager

For additional information about the practices described in this case study, please contact Stacey Knutson, service desk manager, at stacey.knutson@cityofmesa.org.

interact with other department staff and provide the benefit of their experience to other staff.

- **Incorporating help desk staff in customer outreach efforts**—Help desk staff also participate in the city's quarterly users' forum during which the department alerts key users to upcoming software rollouts and other desktop initiatives.
- **Informal communication opportunities for help desk and other staff**—Several times each year, members of the information technology department are invited to the help desk area to meet and talk with the help desk staff. This informal interaction allows staff to get to know one another and discuss issues of common interest in a relaxed setting.

Review every call that could not be resolved immediately

To ensure continuous improvements in help desk service, the department conducts an audit of every call that could not be resolved at the time of the call to determine how a similar call might be handled more quickly in the future. Such audits have led to changes in staff training, team composition, and other customer service functions in the past.

The department also sends an online customer satisfaction survey to all customers upon closure of their help desk request. This feedback is also used to improve help desk operations.

Consult comparative data from peers and industry

Another component of Mesa's continuous improvement efforts is comparison with peers and industry benchmarks. Each year, Mesa compares the performance of its help desk and other information technology activities with that of peers participating in the ICMA Center for Performance Measurement™ (CPM) and with industry benchmarks available from Gartner, Inc., an information technology research and consulting firm.

The department reports its results to the city manager quarterly through the city's MesaStat program, which is modeled on Baltimore's CitiStat program, and annually through the CPM.

County of Pinellas, FL

Performance Indicator

- **Help desk calls resolved at the time of call**

For FY 2006, the county of Pinellas reported that 88 percent of help desk calls were resolved at the time of the call. The mean and median values for all jurisdictions reporting were 43 percent and 38 percent, respectively.

Operating 24 hours a day, seven days a week, the help desk for the county of Pinellas is staffed by 30 in-house employees working in its call center and desktop support center. Three levels of technicians are available to respond to help desk requests, and they are able to take remote control of a user's computer if necessary to resolve the call.

Colocation of call center and desktop support staff

It is Pinellas County's goal to resolve its help desk customers' concerns at the first contact. To that end, in early FY 2006, the county of Pinellas relocated the help desk so that call center staff and desktop technicians could reside in the same facility.

The space is organized so that four senior technicians sit between the call center and desktop support center, allowing call center staff to consult with the senior technicians on complicated tickets. The call center staff members use wireless headsets that allow them to walk (if necessary) to the technicians' desks to seek help.

Although some staff members were initially somewhat apprehensive about the colocation of the call center and the desktop support center, the county has seen a steady increase in its call resolution rate since the change, and staff members now report that they appreciate the benefits of the change.

Cross-training of call center and desktop support staff

To promote speedy resolution of help desk calls further, Pinellas County has also cross-trained some help desk staff. Twenty-five percent of the staff is cross-trained on both call center and desktop technician skills. Also, all desktop technicians spend three weeks working in the call center to enhance their understanding of the call center's work and build relationships with the call center staff.

Pinellas County's information technology department places a strong emphasis on training (both classroom and online formats) and certification. To reinforce this, the department created a "wall of fame" that displays the names and certifications held by team members. The wall is located in a high-traffic area to ensure that it is seen by as many people as possible.

Personal accountability for team success

At the beginning of each fiscal year, all employees work with their supervisors to outline individual goals and objectives for the year. A personal goal and a certification requirement are usually included in each employee's plan. Moreover, each employee's plan must include the team goal of resolving 80

Case Profile

Population:
947,774

Square miles:
280

Median household income:
$40,694

Form of government:
Commission

For additional information about the practices described in this case study, please contact Ray Dilley, senior manager of business technology services, at rdilley@co.pinellas.fl.us.

percent or more of all help desk calls at the time of the call. Performance on this one goal may constitute up to 25 percent of an employee's rating, depending on the employee's job level.

Help desk staff may monitor their own performance on this goal by generating call resolution reports for their calls at any time. Performance reports are published monthly, and they include data on individual and team progress as well as their respective averages. Supervisors are reviewed quarterly and annually.

The county views its ability to resolve 88 percent of help desk calls at the time of the call an opportunity—an opportunity to boost its resolution rate even higher.

City of Westminster, CO

Performance Indicator

- **Overall internal customer satisfaction with general information technology services**

For FY 2006, the city of Westminster's information technology department reported that 90 percent of its customers rated the quality of general information technology services as excellent. (Good, fair, and poor were customers' other rating choices.) The mean and median proportions of customers providing an excellent rating in all other jurisdictions were 49 percent and 48 percent, respectively.

Recruit staff carefully

Westminster officials noted that careful screening for a strong customer service orientation in job candidates is one of the most important factors in ensuring good customer relations. Screening techniques include specific interview questions that are posed to job candidates related to the candidates' views and perceptions of customer service. Also, candidates participate in specific role-playing exercises during the interview that help to highlight interpersonal and customer service abilities.

Westminster staff noted that, although it is possible to teach the technical skills necessary to resolve customers' computer problems, it is much more difficult to teach empathy and congeniality—both of which contribute mightily to success in serving customers frustrated by misbehaving machines.

Incorporate customer feedback into employee evaluations

Westminster's information technology department has been seeking customer feedback regarding its customer service function since the early 1990s.

Each month, the department sends electronic surveys to 20 to 30 customers who received service during the month. The survey requests feedback about each customer's experience with the specific agent who provided assistance; the survey covers the areas of

- Communication
- Cooperation
- Technical knowledge
- Overall satisfaction.

This feedback is used in the individual performance evaluations of the customer service representatives. It is also used to help identify specific areas where each employee may need additional training (for example, on a specific software application, network monitoring, or customer interaction). Employees may also receive special recognition for outstanding service as reported through the customer survey program.

The customer survey results are also used in the aggregate to determine whether the department is hiring qualified people and providing adequate

Case Profile

Population:
109,671

Square miles:
34

Median household income:
$67,094

Form of government:
Council-manager

For additional information about the practices described in this case study, please contact David Puntenney, information technology director, at dpuntenn@ci.westminster.co.us or 303/658-2400, extension 2051.

levels of ongoing technical and interpersonal skill training for employees. Monthly results are posted in the department to help staff maintain focus on the importance of good customer service.

Report results to city officials each year

The department reports annually on this and other performance statistics to the city council and city manager, comparing the city's own performance from year to year and its performance with that of peer communities. The goal of these comparisons is to ensure continuous improvement. (For additional information about Westminster's annual performance-reporting process, please see the Westminster case study in Chapter 1: High Performance Management Practices earlier in this book.)

Library Services

Library Services

City of Albany, OR

Performance Indicator

- **Circulation rate per registered borrower**

For FY 2006, the city of Albany reported circulating 22.1 items per registered borrower. For all jurisdictions reporting that year, the mean rate was 12.4 and the median rate was 11.1.

City supports library acquisitions budget

When asked how the city of Albany was able to achieve such a high circulation rate, the library director stated that library services have enjoyed strong city support—most recently demonstrated by a 25 percent increase in the library's acquisitions budget between FY 2005 and FY 2006.

Attention-getting displays promote circulation

To encourage patrons to pick out books they might not otherwise try, the library began setting up mini displays of popular titles and lesser-known recommendations at the ends of bookshelves—much like the attention-getting, end-of-aisle displays designed to induce impulse buys in grocery stores. Displays are changed monthly to continue stimulating patron interest, and circulation rates indicate that the effort has been successful.

The city of Albany also seeks to boost circulation among special-interest groups. For visually impaired patrons, the library features on its Web site a special display of the latest large-print book, which encourages large-print book circulation.

City incorporates CPM data into its budget and strategic plan

The city is also beginning to incorporate ICMA Center for Performance Measurement™ (CPM) data in its budget document and strategic plan, displaying time-trend data where available.

In the library budget, Albany is also starting to display several CPM indicators. The library director is also considering the implementation of several CPM expenditure-oriented indicators as internal benchmarks.

Case Profile

Population:
46,612

Square miles:
18

Median household income:
$39,409

Form of government:
Council-manager

For additional information about the practices described in this case study, please contact Ed Gallagher, library director, at 541/917-7500 or ed.gallagher@cityofalbany.net.

County of Chesterfield, VA

Case Profile

Population:
278,539

Square miles:
446

Median household income:
$62,384

Form of government:
Council-administrator/manager

For additional information about the practices in this case study, please contact Marshall Lewis, analyst, at lewism@chesterfield.gov.

Performance Indicator

- **Library staffing**

Facing a growing customer population and a static staffing level, the Chesterfield County Public Library explored options for meeting increasing customer service demand by adjusting staffing patterns.

As part of Chesterfield County's emphasis on total quality improvement, the library director appointed a process action team (PAT) to aid the library's administrative team in developing a new staffing plan. The goals of the plan were to

- Accommodate increased customer service demands during peak service hours
- Increase staff efficiency at all times
- Improve customer service generally.

Rigorous data collection

The library's administrative team identified several key performance measures tracked through the ICMA Center for Performance Measurement™ (CPM), Public Library Data Service, and other agencies:

- Circulation per capita
- Staffing per 1,000 population
- Square feet of library space per capita
- Number of facilities or branches per system
- Program attendance
- Annual visitor count
- Annual reference/readers advisory count.

The administrative team then selected several peer libraries that serve populations similar to that of Chesterfield County. The team compared Chesterfield County's performance on each of the key measures with the performance of the peer libraries in order to establish performance targets for Chesterfield.

Effective practice research

The PAT then conducted telephone interviews and site visits with several of the peer libraries to determine which staffing strategies the peer libraries were using to achieve their performance levels.

Synthesis and application of results

On the basis of its research, Chesterfield County determined that it would need at least 12 full-time-equivalent employees to staff an average-sized branch library in its system. The recommended 12 FTEs would need to include one full-time manager, one full-time assistant manager, two full-time degreed librarians, four part-time degreed associate librarians, one full-time customer service supervisor, four customer service FTEs (in a combination of full-time and part-time staff), and one paging-clerical FTE.

Chesterfield County's library staff also developed a number of customer output ratios that can be used to determine when staffing should be increased beyond the recommended complement of 12 FTEs.

City of Corvallis, OR

Case Profile

Population:
53,165

Square miles:
14

Median household income:
$68,100

Form of government:
Council-manager

Performance Indicators

- **Circulation rate per registered borrower**
- **Citizen satisfaction with library services**

For FY 2006, the city of Corvallis reported circulating 29.5 items per registered borrower. For all jurisdictions reporting that year, the mean number of items circulated per registered borrower was 12.4, and the median was 11.1.

That same year, the city also reported that 97 percent of citizens surveyed rated the city's library services as excellent or good. The mean and median proportions of excellent and good ratings for all jurisdictions reporting were 88 percent and 86 percent, respectively.

When asked how the city has achieved such strong circulation rates and customer satisfaction ratings, city officials noted several factors, including:

- Strong commitment to materials acquisition
- Programming tailored by audience, with particularly good results among teen and Spanish-language patrons.

Investment in materials

The city of Corvallis has increased its materials acquisition budget by 3 percent each year since 2003, which allows the library to add new, relevant materials to its collection frequently and, in turn, entices patrons to check out materials and promotes their satisfaction. (Between 1993 and 2003, the Corvallis library was able to increase its materials acquisition budget by 7 percent each year.)

Award-winning programs, tailored by audience

The city has seen its largest circulation growth in its young adult and Spanish-language collections. Between 2003 and 2006, circulation of young adult materials grew by 73 percent, and circulation of Spanish-language materials grew by 11 percent.

To promote interest among teen patrons, the library offers a number of programs, including monthly video game and movie nights.

To reach Spanish-language patrons, the library also offers its monthly Family Fiesta program. The program is intended for the whole family and features storytelling, music, and other activities. Bilingual staff and volunteers are present to assist patrons and encourage registration.

For their outstanding teen programs, two Corvallis librarians recently won an award from the Oregon Young Adult Network. The library also received the Mora Award, which recognizes excellence in library services targeted toward Spanish-language audiences.

Using data to track progress

Like most libraries, the Corvallis library tracks circulation and other statistics carefully. This allows staff to focus materials acquisition funds and other resources in areas of greatest patron interest.

For more information about the practices described in this case study, please contact Teresa P. Landers, deputy library director, at 541/766-6995 or teresa.landers@ci.corvallis.or.us.

The city also shares performance data from the Public Library Data Service and ICMA Center for Performance Measurement™ (CPM) and shows how Corvallis's library service compares with service offered by its peers (in Oregon and across the country). These statistics are provided in Corvallis's annual budget document, strategic plan, and quarterly progress reports.

Note: In addition to the residents of the city of Corvallis, the Corvallis library also serves residents of surrounding Benton County. The population of the library's total service area is 84,125, and its total area is 688 square miles.

City of Davenport, IA

Case Profile

Population:
98,845

Square miles:
66

Median household income:
$42,801

Form of government:
Council-manager

Performance Indicator

- **Citizen satisfaction with library services**

The city of Davenport reported that 91 percent of citizens surveyed rated library services as excellent or good. The mean and median values reported by all other jurisdictions were 88 percent and 86 percent, respectively.

New branch brings patrons back to the library

The city's library director attributes much of this high level of satisfaction to the opening of the city's first permanent branch library in January 2006—but not necessarily in the way that some might think.

Yes, patrons were happy about the new branch, but the library director asserted that the main impact of the new branch was to reintroduce residents to the entire library system, including the main library (see photo).

Since the new branch's opening, patron visits at the main library have increased as well. The increased visitation at the main library has been maintained, so it likely was not just a one-time spike. The director attributes this to patrons becoming aware—through their initial visit to the branch—that the library (both main and branch facilities) offers many services of which they were unaware: DVDs, CDs, and wireless and desktop Internet access.

Leaders emphasize customer service

The director also noted that the mayor, city administrator, and she herself all emphasize high-quality customer service at the city's libraries. Library staff undergo frequent training in communication, customer service, developing relationships with patrons (for example, "Hi, Joe, good to see you again! Did you like that book by Stephen King that I recommended?"), and similar topics.

The library also makes use of comment cards, and the library director deals with customer concerns personally. One example she gave is that a patron complained that the patron-use PCs had dirty keyboards owing largely to the fact that they are almost constantly in use. In response, the library now cleans the keyboards every morning before patrons arrive.

Boosting safety and visibility of children's section helps, too

Another factor to which the library director attributed Davenport's increased patronage and customer satisfaction is the redesign in the fall of 2007 of the main library's interior to make the children's section more visible from both the library entrance (so parents know exactly where it is) and from other areas of the library (to increase the perceived security of the area). Anecdotal evidence suggests a high level of satisfaction from both parents and kids about this change, and the library director reports that usage of the section has increased also.

Walkabouts—when staff get up from behind the desk and start walking around, à la Barnes & Noble—is the next step, coming in August 2008.

For additional information about the practices described in this case study, please contact LaWanda Roudebush, library director, at lroudebush@davenportlibrary.com.

Main Branch of library in Davenport, Iowa. The library was designed by Edward Durrell Stone, who also designed the Kennedy Center in Washington, D.C.

County of Fairfax, VA

Case Profile

Population:
1,067,216

Square miles:
407

Median household income:
$94,610

Form of government:
Council-administrator/manager

Performance Indicator

- **Citizen satisfaction with library services**

Knowing your customers and what they want from their library

The Fairfax County Public Library (FCPL) system uses a variety of survey tools to help understand who its customers are and what kinds of educational, informational, and recreational services they are looking for in their public library.

FCPL seeks to conduct its comprehensive user survey every three to five years (although past surveys have been conducted every four to six years). FCPL also conducts a minimum of two smaller customer surveys annually. All surveys are linked to and support the library's strategic plan.

About the comprehensive user survey

The comprehensive survey asks customers a number of detailed questions regarding their library visits. Questions relate to the frequency and style of library use, reasons for visiting a particular library facility, materials that were sought, activities that were undertaken during the visit, whether staff assistance was requested, resources that were used, satisfaction with the visit, as well as a full set of demographic questions and several open-ended questions.

FCPL usually receives between 7,000 and 9,000 responses to its comprehensive user survey. Survey data are processed using SPSS statistical software, and results are presented to the library's board of trustees, management, and staff. Data are also mined in an ongoing fashion to generate additional insight about patron needs and preferences.

User Survey Retrospective Report, 1984-2006

In 2006, FCPL conducted its fourth comprehensive user survey. It led to the publication of the recent *User Survey Retrospective Report 1984–2006,* which reviewed and compared user survey results over a period of 22 years.

The review indicates that the library is succeeding at meeting patrons' needs:

- 90 percent of respondents to the 2006 survey indicated that they were able to find the materials that they needed while at the library. This may also indicate that the library is stocking the materials of greatest interest to patrons.
- 96 percent of respondents who used the library are receiving the help they need while at the library. Approximately 30 percent of respondents reported requesting help from library staff or volunteers.
- Library users are accessing library materials and services in record numbers. Patron use of a variety of services grew significantly between 2000 and 2006; telephone reference requests grew by 7 percent; in-library Internet use grew by 8 percent; use of the FCPL Web site grew by 76 percent.

For more information about the practices described in this case study, please contact Doug Miller, assistant library coordinator, at douglas.miller@fairfaxcounty.gov.

Given the high levels of community use and customer satisfaction with the FCPL, it appears the library is fulfilling its mission

> . . . to enrich individual and community life by providing and encouraging the use of library resources and services to meet the evolving education, recreational and informational needs of the residents of Fairfax County and Fairfax City.

and taking strides toward fulfilling its vision of being

> . . . the dynamic link connecting customers to local and global resources for lifelong learning and self-enrichment.

City of Johnson City, TN

Case Profile

Population:
61,233

Square miles:
41

Median household income:
$30,835

Form of government:
Council-manager

Performance Indicator

- **Citizen satisfaction with library services**

For FY 2006, the city of Johnson City reported that 97 percent of citizens surveyed rated library services as excellent or good. The mean and median values for all jurisdictions reporting were 88 percent and 86 percent, respectively.

Semiautonomous organization promotes quick responses to customers

Located north of the city's downtown district, the Johnson City Public Library is a 501(c)(3) nonprofit corporation. As a component unit of the city, the library receives 85 percent of its funding from the Johnson City government and 6 percent from the local county government, and it generates 9 percent on its own through fines, fees, and donations.

The Johnson City Public Library sets its own budget, pays its own bills, and processes its own payroll. It has a dedicated administrative staff to handle the business of the library, a facility manager to maintain the building and grounds, and an information technology specialist who keeps the library current in equipment, software, and operating systems.

The library's facility manager takes pride in maintaining the clean, well-lit building, and all staff members go to great lengths to maintain a comfortable and inviting environment.

Staff members suggest this independence has had a direct impact on the high ratings the library has received from citizens. Concerns and problems can be addressed immediately by either the administrative staff, the facility manager, or the IT specialist, thereby limiting the service disruptions or facility maintenance issues that affect library patrons. The library's facility manager takes pride in maintaining the clean, well-lit building, and all staff members go to great lengths to maintain a comfortable and inviting environment.

The library's IT specialist diligently works to maintain the library's software and hardware. A state-mandated three-year technology plan has driven the IT specialist to look for grant money to help make the money in the library's operating budget stretch further. Computers are kept updated with uniform operating systems and programs, and the library is outfitted with wireless Internet and flat-screen monitors on all public computers.

The Johnson City Public Library also has very low turnover among staff members. Patrons are able to rely on the library staff and their abilities to answer questions about materials and technology.

Services tailored by age group and other patron preferences

Staff point to the diverse array of programs provided at the Johnson City Public Library as another key to the library's success at receiving high

For additional information about the practices described in this case study, please contact Cathy Griffith, assistant director for administrative service at Johnson City Public Library, at cgriffith@jcpl.net.

ratings from citizens for library services. Programs are available in the youth services department for all age groups—from "Two's Company" for 2-year-olds, to "Mystery Night" for teens, to "Family Storytimes" held every Monday evening for families. The library also offers a bilingual storytime for Spanish-language patrons. In addition to these regular programs, each summer is a different adventure for youth and teens as the library presents its summer reading program. Special programs are presented every Thursday throughout the summer and are so well attended that they had to be broken up into two sessions, one in the morning and another in the afternoon.

Adults also enjoy tailored programming at the Johnson City Public Library. Book discussion groups meet for "Tales and Talk." Local genealogists utilize the library's Tennessee Room and local history resources to find ancestors or create a family tree. Each year special programs are scheduled in conjunction with Women's History Month, Black History Month, and National Library Week. In addition to these programs, an outreach librarian attends community events to promote library services.

Inviting the public in

The Johnson City Public Library has a meeting center that accommodates up to 130 people and is heavily used by the community. It features state-of-the-art audiovisual equipment, large projection screens, and Internet service.

With all that they have to offer, library staff continue to communicate with patrons to gauge their satisfaction with and interest in the programmatic offerings, and staff adjust programs accordingly.

City of Wilsonville, OR

Case Profile

Population:
16,510

Square miles:
7

Median household income:
$52,512

Form of government:
Council-manager

Performance Indicator

- **Circulation rates per registered borrower**

For FY 2006, the city of Wilsonville reported a circulation rate of 30.6 items per registered borrower. For all jurisdictions reporting that year, the mean was 12.4, and the median was 11.1.

Patron-centered services encourage circulation

The city of Wilsonville attributes its high circulation rate to several factors:

- **Convenient online services**—The library offers extensive online services, including 24-hour catalog access, downloadable audio books, and a renewal reminder service (which alerts patrons by e-mail three days before their materials are due). Patrons may also renew their materials online, which promotes not only better circulation but also, more important, greater patron convenience.
- **Attractive, comfortable facilities**—The city's main library building features an extensive collection, numerous fine art displays, wireless Internet access, comfortable seating, and a large amount of free parking, all of which are intended to attract patrons and encourage circulation of materials.
- **Enticing book displays**—Wilsonville's library also features numerous displays in the lobby and throughout the library, at the ends of shelves and elsewhere, that include books, book reviews, and other items intended to encourage patron selections.
- **Effective publicity**—Since the early 1990s, the Wilsonville public library has had a biweekly column in the local newspaper, which it uses to promote programs, advertise interesting titles, and attract patron interest generally—all of which positively influence circulation.
- **Extensive hours thanks to volunteers**—The library also can remain open as long as it does each day because it makes effective use of volunteers. Volunteers' hours allow the library to stay open more hours, which in turn allows more materials to circulate.

Children's collection contributes to circulation performance

The public library of the city of Wilsonville also boasts a wide selection of children's materials, which draws in families and helps promote strong circulation for children's materials (including books, CDs, and movies). Children's materials comprise approximately one-third of the library's overall circulation.

City shares performance indicators in annual budget

The Wilsonville library reports its performance on a number of indicators—including circulation, reference transactions, and more—in the city's annual budget document. The city also compares its performance with the average for all libraries in the state of Oregon.

For additional information about the practices described in this case study, please contact Patrick Duke, library director, at 503/570-1590 or duke@ci.wilsonville.or.us

Parks and Recreation

Parks and Recreation

City of Coral Springs, FL

Performance Indicator

- **Citizen ratings of the quality of parks and recreation programs**

For FY 2006, 95 percent of the residents surveyed rated the quality of Coral Springs's parks and recreation programs as excellent or good. For all jurisdictions reporting, the mean and median values were 79 percent and 77 percent, respectively.

Knowing and responding to your customer: it's as easy as 1-2-3!

1. Survey, survey, and survey again
2. Break the results apart and look for trends
3. Change it up!

Data are reviewed as a whole, but also by age group and specific park. By reviewing the data in this manner, the city can better respond to the needs of patron groups.

Survey, survey, and survey again

Point of service surveys coupled with the city's biennial resident survey help Coral Springs stay accountable in its commitment to high-quality parks and recreation programs. To ensure that citizen feedback is solicited regularly, evaluation forms are distributed at all recreation programs. Every quarter department staff administer the surveys in person at sites throughout the city. By doing so, staff have the opportunity to speak with program attendees about their experiences with the city's programmatic offerings, whether they are praiseworthy or need improvement.

Break the results apart and look for trends

Not only does Coral Springs survey residents regularly, but the city also segments the data. Data are reviewed as a whole, but also by age group and specific park. By reviewing the data in this manner, the city can better respond to the needs of patron groups as well as set appropriate staffing and enrollment standards. One input the city relies on heavily in this analysis is revenue, as it is seen as an indicator of satisfaction; the city becomes concerned about customer satisfaction if revenues dip without another explanation such as a decrease in fees charged for specific activities.

Change it up!

The biennial survey provides the city with the opportunity to ask citizens about their perceptions of overall recreation programming, whereas the point of service evaluations allow parks and recreation staff to ask end users about their experiences. By segmenting data and reviewing the data nearly in real time, Coral Springs is positioned to, and frequently chooses to,

Case Profile

Population:
131,257

Square miles:
24

Median household income:
$63,197

Form of government:
Council-manager

For more information about the practices described in this case study, please contact Rick Engle, director of parks and recreation, at 954/345-2110.

alter programs in response to feedback. If a program is less than favorably received, the city modifies or replaces it. Through a new point-of-service survey, the city then asks attendees to evaluate the new program and modify it further as necessary.

City of Henderson, NV

Performance Indicators

- **Citizen ratings of overall satisfaction with parks and recreation services**
- **Citizen ratings of the quality of parks and recreation programs**

For FY 2006, the city of Henderson's parks and recreation department reported that 95 percent of its customers rated overall satisfaction with department services as excellent or good. The mean and median values for all jurisdictions reporting were 81 percent and 73 percent, respectively.

With regard to the quality of programs specifically, 90 percent of respondents gave a rating of excellent or good. The mean value for all jurisdictions reporting was 79 percent; the median was 77 percent.

"A place to call home"

Located in southeastern Nevada, not far from the hustle and bustle of Las Vegas, Henderson bills itself as "A place to call home." The city's parks and recreation department seeks to typify this ideal through the provision of beautiful outdoor spaces and other recreation amenities.

Beautiful parks enhance the hometown atmosphere

The city of Henderson boasts a robust park system supported by a team of ornamental horticulturalists and other professionals who cultivate the natural beauty of the city's parks. With approximately 300 days of sunshine each year, Henderson offers many opportunities for outdoor activity—and the city's parks are frequently the center.

An example of Henderson's parks facilities.

Case Profile

Population:
257,838

Square miles:
98

Median household income:
$56,857

Form of government:
Council-manager

For additional information about the practices described in this case study, please contact Mary Ellen Donner, director of parks and recreation, at maryellen.donner@cityofhenderson.com or 702/267-4000.

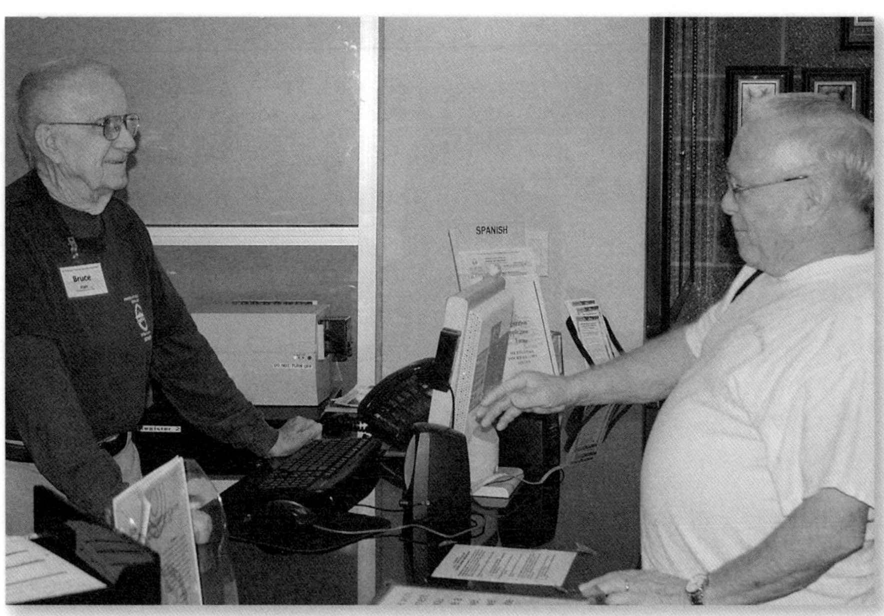

Henderson staff member assists a parks and recreation patron.

Seek, develop, and support credentialed staff

To ensure that its parks are well maintained and appealing to visitors, Henderson actively recruits experienced, degreed horticulturalists and offers full tuition reimbursement to all full-time employees pursuing degrees related to their positions. The city also encourages staff to seek and maintain memberships in professional associations.

The city cultivates a steady supply of highly qualified new staff by offering internships to college students pursuing degrees related to parks and recreation. Henderson's internship program, known as one of the best in the area, boasts

- Above-average pay
- One-on-one time with managers
- Flexible work arrangements designed to accommodate students' schedules.

Cultivate and reward good customer service

To ensure that park visitors and recreation customers receive good customer service, the department during interviews screens potential employees for a good attitude toward customer service and provides employees with ongoing customer service training.

Employees cited for good customer service on the job are rewarded with paid time away from work. Rewards begin with long lunch periods and may advance as high as a fully paid day away from work.

The Henderson parks and recreation department uses customer survey data in budget requests and bond proposals and shares the data at council meetings, in press releases, and through other outlets.

County of Miami-Dade, FL

Performance Indicator

- **Citizen ratings of the quality of parks and recreation programs**

For FY 2006, Miami–Dade County's parks and recreation department reported that 93 percent of the citizens surveyed rated the quality of parks and recreation programs as excellent or good. The mean and median values for all jurisdictions reporting were 79 percent and 77 percent, respectively.

Create a sense of community

Perhaps a result of the favorable climate and access to the outdoors, participation in parks and recreation programs is woven into the lives of many residents in Miami–Dade County. It is not uncommon for parents to send their children to the very recreation programs they attended as youngsters or for camp participants to later seek employment with the county's parks and recreation department. The parks and recreation department works hard to maintain the county's facilities and provide the quality programs to which residents are accustomed.

Price services competitively

To ensure that participation is accessible to as many residents as possible, Miami–Dade emphasizes the importance of pricing fee-based programs moderately. The department also offers reduced fees and scholarship programs to assist lower-income families. No child is turned away from a parks and recreation program because of inability to pay.

Partner with local organizations to boost recreational opportunities

Many of the parks and recreation department's specialty programs are undertaken with private sector partners and at some of the county's unique facilities. Sports programs, for example, are often conducted with support from local nonprofit organizations with national affiliations, such as the American Youth Soccer Organization, US Club Soccer, and the National Association for Youth Sports. At Miami Metrozoo, the Zoological Society of Florida provides education programs on behalf of the department.

Cultivate staff (and their skills)

Harking back to the example of many participants in the county's children's camps later becoming counselors, Miami–Dade's parks and recreation department attributes much of its success in achieving high citizen satisfaction ratings to its committed staff. A number of paid staff also boast histories as volunteers with the department.

The department also notes that all staff undergo initial background checks and drug screening, with rescreening each year.

Permanent staff (but not seasonal staff) also participate in the county's health, safety, and professional skills training courses, which are based on the U.S. Navy's benefits-based programming model. The training programs

Case Profile

Population:
2,246,848

Square miles:
1,964

Median household income:
$37,418

Form of government:
Council-administrator/manager

For additional information about the practices described in this case study, please contact Roger Lewis, parks and recreation strategic planning, at rlp@miamidade.gov.

include general health and safety topics, recreation planning, and program management. Staff complete 13 modules over the course of two years.

Craft innovative programs

The Miami–Dade parks and recreation department seeks to offer a wide range of programs that appeal to many audiences while managing financial and personnel resources well.

"Fit to Play, Fun for Life" is a particularly popular program, one that may be among those that citizens think of when they give such high satisfaction ratings. Developed for the FY 2006 program year, "Fit to Play, Fun for Life" is a 10-week summer program that teaches children healthy eating and exercise habits and involves the whole family.

The county also offers programs tailored for other groups like senior citizens and patrons with developmental disabilities.

Inspect for success

Because the condition of the facilities directly affects the experiences of the attendees, the county created the Sparkle Tour to ensure facilities are well maintained and can serve the county's parks and recreation programs well. Under the terms of the program, park managers inspect their facilities each week, regional managers inspect their facilities each month, and assistant directors inspect each quarter. Twice a year, the director of the Miami–Dade parks and recreation department also invites employees from other county departments to accompany parks and recreation staff on a Sparkle Tour. These outside staff help to provide a more well-rounded view of park conditions, and they sometimes encourage useful changes.

Track and report results regularly

The Miami–Dade parks and recreation department uses organizationwide balanced scorecards. The performance measures for the parks and recreation department are closely monitored, and the department's progress toward the targets is posted to the county's Web site at the end of every quarter.

Police Services

Police Services

City of Bellevue, WA

Performance Indicator

- **Citizen rating of police contact quality**

For FY 2006, the city of Bellevue reported that 86 percent of citizens rated the quality of contact with police as excellent or good. The mean and median values for all jurisdictions reporting were 80 percent and 79 percent, respectively.

The city of Bellevue reports that it employs a personal approach for ensuring good relationships with citizens:

- Responding to all calls in person, whenever possible
- Keeping citizens informed regarding complaint resolution
- Providing many opportunities for citizens to report their concerns (911, local stations, patrol officers, an online traffic problem reporting system, and more).

City staff also take pride in noting that in addition to receiving high marks for general satisfaction among citizens having contact with the police department, department staff also receive strong survey ratings specifically for their professionalism.

If a long wait time is expected for an in-person response to a 911 call, dispatch staff will contact the caller and provide an update regarding the status of the response

Take the perspective of the resident

City staff state that Bellevue's police department considers itself a service-oriented agency. As a reflection of this service orientation, the department encourages in-person responses to all 911 calls, regardless of the reason for the call.

The city's service orientation also applies to its dispatch operation. If a long wait time is expected for an in-person response to a 911 call, dispatch staff will contact the caller and provide an update regarding the status of the response (with the information that, for example, a patrol car is on its way). Upon arrival, officers spend as much time as possible with residents in order to understand their concerns and provide reassurance.

Foster relationships with the community

Neighborhood patrol operations include vehicle patrols, bicycle patrols, and fixed station officers, all of whom share the goal of fostering close relationships between the patrol officers and local residents and businesses.

Police officers also work together with other city staff (for example, parks department, code enforcement) to address neighborhood concerns about drug activity, teen hangouts, and other issues.

Case Profile

Population:
117,000

Square miles:
32

Median household income:
$69,880

Form of government:
Council-manager

For additional information about the practices described in this case study, please contact Rich Siegel, performance and outreach coordinator, at rcsiegel@bellevuewa.gov.

Patrol officers in Bellevue usually carry small individual caseloads, allowing time to follow up on prior calls. The officers keep citizens up-to-date on how their complaints are being resolved, which reinforces the message that citizens' concerns are important to the department and receive attention.

In addition to regular neighborhood patrol activities, the department and residents also benefit from the assistance of its community service unit, comprising 76 volunteers who carry out tasks from clerical support at neighborhood stations to assistance with monitoring of handicapped parking spaces.

Bellevue also holds a community police academy twice a year where residents can learn about community and neighborhood policing strategies. The program includes ride-alongs with officers so residents can see firsthand how officers patrol their neighborhoods.

Provide various outlets for feedback

The Bellevue police department also has a specialized traffic unit with a strong commitment to traffic enforcement and accident investigation. The unit invites residents to submit reports of traffic problems like obscured street signs, recurring instances of speeding vehicles, and other concerns through its online assistance system accessible through the city's Web site. The department responds to requests with the help of traffic engineers and other city staff—and then informs residents about the resolution.

Seek to improve further

The department is pleased with its citizen satisfaction results, but it continues to seek ways to improve relations with residents.

The department is also working on improving communication within the department, which should in turn further promote good relationships with citizens. A number of initiatives are under way to facilitate internal communication, including meetings at each level of the organization to discuss policies, monthly online video messages from the chief to all department staff, and online departmental newsletters.

City of Cumberland, MD

Performance Indicators

- Total response time in minutes to top-priority calls
- Percentage of UCR Part I violent crimes cleared

For FY 2006, the city of Cumberland reported a total response time to top-priority calls of 4.33 minutes. The mean and median values for all jurisdictions reporting were 6.8 minutes and 6.7 minutes, respectively.

With regard to UCR Part I violent crimes, Cumberland reported clearing 92 percent. The mean and median values for all jurisdictions reporting were 53.9 percent and 53.1 percent, respectively.

Establish patrol zones

The police department for the city of Cumberland attributes much of its success on both indicators to the implementation of zone-based patrols.

The city is divided into four patrol zones, each covering about three square miles. The zones were established taking geography and road conditions into consideration. Care was also taken to ensure that all police responses within a zone could be made as quickly and effectively as possible.

Patrol officers receive permanent assignment to one of the four zones. The permanent assignments help officers come to know their zones well; officers build relationships with residents and develop an understanding of potential issues. The city also has several officers who circulate among the zones to cover calls during peak periods and provide backup as needed.

Work as a team within the department and the larger community

The city of Cumberland also notes that patrol officers play an important role in ensuring clearance of violent crimes in the city. Although it is the detectives who usually close such cases, Cumberland's patrol officers play an important role by conducting thorough preliminary investigations, gathering evidence, and collecting accounts from residents, which in turn promote good outcomes for the detectives who take on the cases.

The city of Cumberland also participates in a regional criminal investigation task force, which helps boost its violent crime clearance rate. Comprising detectives from the city of Cumberland and other law enforcement agencies in the area, the Allegany County Combined Criminal Investigation (C3I) Unit consults and assists city police officers with investigations and court preparation. Moreover, the C3I Unit provides police officers in the city of Cumberland with specialized equipment and personnel (like forensic tools and expertise) important to the outcome of many investigations.

Case Profile

Population:
121,518

Square miles:
10

Median household income:
$25,142

Form of government:
Council-manager

For additional information about the practices described in this case study, please contact Jeffrey Rhodes, director of administrative services, at jrhodes@allconet.org.

City of Eugene, OR

Case Profile

Population:
146,160

Square miles:
43

Median household income:
$33,070

Form of government:
Council-manager

Performance Indicator

- **Citizen rating of safety of their neighborhoods after dark**

For FY 2006, the city of Eugene reported that 87 percent of survey respondents indicated that they felt very safe or reasonably safe in their neighborhoods after dark. The mean and median figures for all jurisdictions reporting were 76 percent and 70 percent, respectively.

When asked how the city of Eugene promotes a feeling of safety among residents in their neighborhoods, the police department made special note of two programs:

- Eugene's crime prevention unit
- "Eugene VIP" volunteer program.

Staff also noted that the city enjoys relatively peaceful farm, forest, and small-city surroundings.

Connect with citizens through active, nonsworn crime prevention units

The city's crime prevention unit is staffed by nonsworn, uniformed police personnel who patrol on foot and by bicycle, speaking with residents and business owners, encouraging personal safety, and learning about neighborhood and business district concerns. Four units are stationed throughout the city to ensure that unit staff are able to make connections with as many residents as possible.

The Eugene police department also boasts a highly mobilized volunteer force that provides more than $100,000 worth of staff time to the department each year.

City staff note that Eugene has a lower-than-average ratio of sworn police officers to residents, but that feelings of personal safety among residents remain high. They attribute this in part to the city's broad use of civilian crime prevention personnel.

Empower citizens through meaningful volunteer policing opportunities

The Eugene police department also boasts a highly mobilized volunteer force that provides more than $100,000 worth of staff time to the department each year. Volunteers are recruited and assigned through the department's Volunteers in Policing (VIP) program; approximately 85 volunteers currently serve. As a testament to the program's success, Eugene employs a full-time, paid staff person just to coordinate police department volunteers.

As noted in the city's citation as a 2006 winner of the Outstanding Achievement in Law Enforcement Volunteer Programs Award, awarded by the International Association of Chiefs of Police and Science Applications International Corporation, Eugene police department volunteers serve in a

For additional information about the practices described in this case study, please contact Captain Pete Kerns, police department, at 541/682-5252 or pete.m.kerns@ci.eugene.or.us.

number of capacities, many directly supporting crime prevention and case resolution activities:

- Assist with warrant verifications
- Staff neighborhood substations
- Dispose of confiscated property
- Perform radar patrol
- Enforce regulations setting aside parking spaces for the disabled.

Eugene's police department volunteers also engage in other office support and administrative tasks. The city's Web site notes that new volunteer assignments may be crafted to meet the interests and educational goals of prospective volunteers.

City staff suggest that incorporating volunteers in so many capacities within the police department helps to demonstrates Eugene's commitment to community policing. The practice also empowers the volunteers themselves to promote safety in their community.

City of Highland Park, IL

Case Profile

Population:
31,365

Square miles:
12.5

Median household income:
$100,967

Form of government:
Council-manager

Performance Indicator

- **Citizen rating of safety of their neighborhoods after dark**

For FY 2006, 97 percent of residents responding to a Highland Park citizen satisfaction survey reported that they felt "very safe" or "reasonably safe" in their neighborhoods after dark. The mean and median values for all jurisdictions reporting were 76 and 70 percent, respectively.

City officials cited several factors that they believe contribute to citizens' positive perceptions of neighborhood safety in Highland Park:

- **Strong communication plan**—Highland Park uses the latest technology to communicate with residents by the most efficient and appropriate means in each situation:
  - — Reverse 911 and text messaging to alert residents in emergency situations
  - — E-mail to announce time-sensitive but less important information
  - — Monthly city newsletter and newspaper announcements to communicate about issues that are important for wide release but less time sensitive.

  Requests for residents to update contact information are regularly published in the city's monthly newsletter. Residents are encouraged to list cell phone numbers and alternate e-mail addresses. The city Web site also encourages residents to sign up for text and e-mail alerts via the city's Web site.

- **Permanent shift assignments**—To build trust and confidence between residents and officers (which in turn promotes safety), Highland Park assigns officers to their shifts on a permanent basis.
- **Collaboration with code enforcement**—The police department works closely with the city's code enforcement staff to ensure that junk vehicles, graffiti, and other problems that can diminish feelings of safety in neighborhoods are addressed quickly. This spirit of interdepartmental cooperation pervades the city staff, increasing staff effectiveness and promoting citizen satisfaction.
- **Officers who reflect community values**—The city also seeks to recruit officers who represent the values of the community, which further helps to promote good relationships with residents. One example is education: Most Highland Park adults have college degrees, and the department seeks officers with similar educational backgrounds. Nearly 60 percent of Highland Park's officers hold bachelor's degrees, and 8 percent have master's degrees.

Highland Park seeks to ensure that its police officers have a visible presence in the city's neighborhoods—making them accessible to residents and helping to deter criminal activity.

For additional information about the practices described in this case study, please contact Patrick Brennan, deputy city manager, at 847/926-1003 or pbrennan@cityhpil.com.

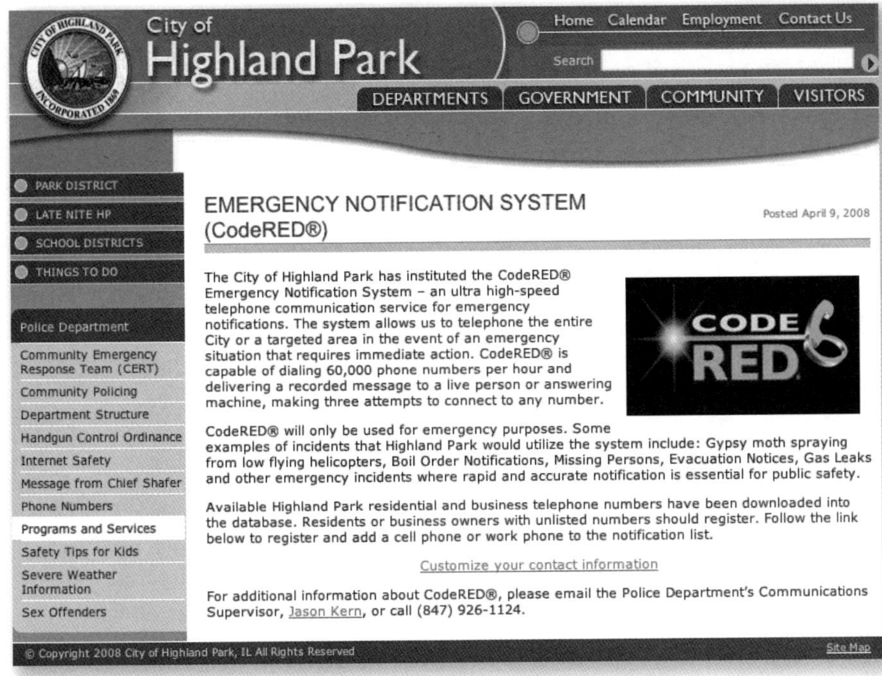

Web page for citizen signup for emergency notification system, Highland Park, Illinois.

City of Johnson City, TN

Case Profile

Population:
61,233

Square miles:
41

Median household income:
$30,835

Form of government:
Council-manager

Performance Indicator

- **Citizen rating of police contact quality**

For FY 2006, the city of Johnson City reported that 80 percent of citizens rated the quality of contact with police as excellent or good. The mean and median values for all jurisdictions reporting were 80 percent and 79 percent, respectively.

The city of Johnson City points to the quality of its staff as a main contributor to its high satisfaction ratings from citizens. The department also cites its relentless pursuit of facts and careful enforcement of the law within a community policing framework.

Recruit and train officers to treat residents like family

With a department motto of "the best serving the best," the Johnson City police department encourages its officers to treat residents in the same manner that they would want members of their own families treated. The department also trains officers in how to interact with residents effectively and courteously. The training is also presented as a networking opportunity where officers can build professional relationships that will provide mutual support for good communication with residents over time.

Build–and maintain–relationships with residents

Officers receive permanent beat assignments, allowing them to develop close relationships with residents. In fact, many officers happily report that they are on a first-name basis with residents on their beats. They also report that citizens frequently approach to ask questions or voice concerns.

City staff report that many police officers, the chief included, often make their mobile phone numbers available to residents so that the residents may share with police any helpful information about emerging issues. The city has found that this practice facilitates effective community policing.

Johnson City also actively promotes opportunities for officers to interact with citizens outside of crime investigation and other direct policing situations. One such opportunity is the citizen police academy program. Johnson City operates two citizen police academy sessions each year and since 1992 has graduated nearly 1,000 residents.

The city also offers a junior police academy, which teaches children and youth about law enforcement. This has served as a springboard for some who became interested in pursuing policing as a career.

The goal of both academies is to encourage communication between residents and the department and help citizens feel that they are partners with the police in ensuring the community's well-being.

Share information with residents

The police department also promotes positive interactions with citizens by sharing as much information with them as possible. The Johnson City police

For additional information about the practices described in this case study, please contact John D. Lowry, chief of police, at jdlowry@johnsoncitytn.org.

department uses computer crime mapping to show trends in different neighborhoods and policing districts within the city. The data are analyzed daily, weekly, and monthly. Results are discussed at staff meetings, and plans for addressing concerns are designed and evaluated.

Police department representatives often bring crime maps to neighborhood association and community meetings, helping residents to see trends and inviting their assistance in resolving issues. The Johnson City police department asserts that both internal and external communication help build trust and confidence with residents and are essential to serving the community well.

Build relationships with community organizations

The department also seeks to promote positive impressions among community members by building relationships with community groups like the media and community and neighborhood associations.

The city equips its officers with wireless personal digital assistants with which they submit incident reports from the field.

For the past several years, the department has hosted a media luncheon that has been attended by local broadcast and print media representatives, police department officials, and city administration. The luncheon provides an opportunity for members of the media and representatives of the department and the city to discuss issues of mutual concern and better understand each others' roles, with the goal of working together for the benefit of the community.

The city also has approximately 12 active neighborhood associations, several of which have a neighborhood watch component. The police department sends a representative to nearly every meeting, and the chief himself attends as many as his schedule allows. The department finds the neighborhood meetings helpful as another tool for promoting positive contact with residents. The police department has a dedicated public relations officer who helps coordinate work with the neighborhood associations.

Equip officers with PDAs for rapid response in the field

To encourage quick processing of information about crimes and other issues requiring a police response, the city equips its officers with wireless personal digital assistants (PDAs) with which they submit incident reports from the field. Many police departments equip officers with laptops in the field, but Johnson City has found PDAs to be a better field-based solution than laptops because the PDAs are

- Less expensive
- Smaller and lighter in weight (they fit in the palm of the hand)
- Not tied to the police vehicle.

The department has also found that the amount of time required for an officer to file an incident report has substantially decreased with the use of the PDAs. As a result, officers have more time to patrol their beats, making contact with residents and business owners and engaging in other community policing activities.

City of Mesa, AZ

Performance Indicator

- **Response time in minutes to top-priority calls**

For FY 2006, the city of Mesa reported that it was able to respond to top-priority police calls in an average of 3.7 minutes. This includes the time from receipt of call to arrival on the scene. The mean and median values for all other jurisdictions reporting were 6.8 minutes and 6.7 minutes, respectively.

Manage on the basis of evidence; Mesa adapted CompStat model

The Mesa police department attributes its excellent response time to rigorous collection and application of performance information.

Using an evidence-based management system adapted from the CompStat Plus program developed by the Los Angeles police department (which in turn is based on New York City's CompStat program), the Mesa police department conducts rigorous monthly reviews of policing performance on a variety of indicators, including response time. The monthly reviews begin with written submission of performance statistics to the police chief; this is followed by an in-person meeting attended by the chief, assistant department chiefs, geographic district chiefs, and support personnel. The meetings are open to the public and the media. Most last approximately four hours.

To ensure the ability to respond quickly, the city maintains the ability to redraw its police districts as often as once each year.

During the monthly review meetings, performance data are presented and used to stimulate discussion about successes and improvement targets within the department. It is important to note that it is the improvement-oriented discussion—not the data—that is considered the product of this review process.

By closely monitoring performance in this fashion, the department is able to track progress toward objectives and shift resources to respond to changing priorities.

Examine districting plan periodically; redistrict as needed

One item that is watched particularly closely during this monthly review process (and constant district-level monitoring) is response time.

Recent reviews showed a decline in response times in the city's eastern police district. Through further study, staff determined that the decline was due to growing traffic congestion along the main north-south corridor in the district. The decline was further attributed to the fact that the eastern district covers a much larger area than the city's other three policing districts.

To ensure the ability to respond quickly to such concerns, the city maintains the ability to redraw its police districts as often as once each year. This

Case Profile

Population:
455,984

Square miles:
131

Median household income:
$44,861

Form of government:
Council-manager

For additional information about the practices described in this case study, please contact Detective Stephen Badger, at 480/644-3670, or stephen.badger@cityofmesa.org.

is currently under consideration for the eastern district. One redrawing option under consideration is dividing the current district into two new ones.

Minimize dispatch time

Dispatch operators are also required to transmit all top-priority call information to officers within two minutes of receiving such a call. A subset of top-priority calls, known as Priority E calls (which involve threat to life), must be dispatched within one minute. In both cases, these standards are intended to minimize response time and save lives and property.

Mesa officials also note that city streets are laid in a uniform grid pattern, which facilitates finding addresses and routing around traffic problems when necessary.

Village of Skokie, IL

Performance Indicator

- **Citizen rating of safety of their neighborhoods after dark**

In FY 2006, 87 percent of citizen survey respondents indicated that they felt "very safe" or "reasonably safe" in their Skokie neighborhoods after dark. The mean and median values for all jurisdictions reporting were 76 and 70 percent, respectively.

Promote neighborhood safety with high touch approach

To foster feelings of safety among village residents, the Skokie police department employs a "high touch" approach, interacting with citizens as much as possible, not just when crimes occur but in as many positive situations as possible:

- **Active volunteer program**—The Skokie police department has an active volunteer program, with 75 residents currently on the roster. The volunteers provide significant help during village festivals by serving as greeters and assisting village staff. The volunteers also serve as scenario actors during the citizen police academy. In addition, volunteers assist with some office work, traffic safety programs, and other low-risk projects.
- **Robust neighborhood watch program**—Skokie boasts of having 5,000 residents involved in 160 neighborhood watch blocks. At least a portion of every neighborhood in the village is covered by one of Skokie's neighborhood watch groups. Each block in the program has a block captain who meets with representatives from the department at least twice per year (or more often depending on circumstances). By having block captains—as opposed to neighborhood captains—the police are able to develop close working relationships with participants.
- **Popular citizen and youth police academies**—A total of 60 citizens participate in two annual Citizen Police Academy sessions. The Citizen Police Academy addresses such topics as criminal and civil law, DUI countermeasures, patrol procedures, the canine program, the use of force, public safety telecommunications, the police as social worker role, and illicit drug and gang suppression.

  The Youth Police Academy also serves 60 participants in two sessions each year. This academy introduces the participants to the police department in general and offers classes in police, fire, and EMS systems; traffic orientation; bicycle safety; drugs and gangs; and safe driving. Each academy session ends with a swimming pool party and graduation ceremony.
- **Follow-up calls**—The village also follows up with citizens by telephone when contact with the police department is recorded in order to ensure that the situation was resolved to the satisfaction of the citizen.
- **Home security checks**—The police department offers free home visits from officers upon request to assess physical security aspects like lighting, landscaping, and lock integrity.

Case Profile

Population:
64,678

Square miles:
10

Median household income:
$57,375

Form of government:
Council-manager

For additional information about the practices described in this case study, please contact Deputy Chief Russ Van at russ.van@skokie.org.

The department believes that these efforts pay dividends in two major ways:

- They boost officers' presence in the community, which may help to deter crime.
- They foster positive relationships between officers and community members, which may facilitate the solving of crimes when crimes do occur.

Build trust with new immigrants

The Skokie police department also employs tailored communication methods to reach out to the many new immigrant families living in the village. Because some recent immigrants in Skokie have come from countries where police and other government officials were not friendly to residents, Skokie is making special efforts to build trust with them:

- **Project SAFE**—Modeled on drug abuse resistance education (DARE) but tailored to meet the needs of Skokie's diverse population of longtime residents and recent immigrants, Project SAFE offers children and youth instruction in personal and family safety. One major aim of the program is to demonstrate to new residents that police in Skokie can be trusted and depended upon to help them.
- **International Citizens Academy**—This academy introduces police concepts to newer residents of Skokie. Approximately 30 residents (the majority of whom were born outside of the United States) participated in the most recent academy. Although the topics are very similar to the conventional citizen police academy, the presentations are made from an international perspective, with an emphasis on the open nature of policing in the United States (for example, the evolution of constitutional restraints on the use of force, arrest, and search).

The motto of the Skokie police department is "People are our profession," and through its many outreach efforts, the department puts this motto into practice every day.

City of St. Charles, IL

Performance Indicator

- **Percentage of UCR Part I violent crimes cleared**

In FY 2006, the city of St. Charles reported clearing 82 percent of violent crime cases. The mean and median clearance rates for all jurisdictions reporting were 54 percent and 53 percent, respectively.

Delegate authority to boost clearance rate

The St. Charles police department cites as the greatest contributor to its high clearance rate for violent crimes the authority that it delegates to patrol officers to solve crimes themselves when they are able to do so. Only the toughest cases are referred to the investigations unit. (The department requires that all cases involving aggravated sexual assault and homicide be referred to investigations.)

By working as an integrated team, patrol officers and investigators are able to focus their resources more efficiently while also providing more effective outcomes for the residents of St. Charles.

This delegation of investigatory authority boosts the clearance rate in two ways:

- It promotes rapid closure of less complicated cases at the patrol level.
- It allows investigators to dedicate more resources to the most complicated cases, ostensibly promoting more efficient closure of them as well.

Key to making this arrangement work is the high level of cooperation and teamwork between patrol officers and investigators. By working as an integrated team, they are able to focus their resources more efficiently while also providing more effective outcomes for the residents of St. Charles.

Delegate authority to increase job satisfaction

In addition to promoting resolution of a high proportion of cases, St. Charles officials note that allowing patrol officers to solve many of their own cases has a major side benefit: it boosts job satisfaction among patrol officers. Officers appreciate the opportunity to see many of their cases through to the end rather than having to forward all of them to someone else to solve.

Allowing patrol officers to solve cases also prepares many for transition into the investigations unit.

Case Profile

Population:
31,834

Square miles:
15

Median household income:
$69,424

Form of government:
Council-manager

For additional information about the practices described in this case study, please contact Detective Sergeant Steve Huffman at 630/443-3732 or shuffman@stcharlesil.gov.

Purchasing

Purchasing

City of Reno, NV

Performance Indicators

- **Customer satisfaction with the quality of service**
- **Customer satisfaction with the timeliness of service**

For FY 2006, Reno reported that 93 percent of customers surveyed rated the quality of purchasing services as excellent or good. The mean and median values for all jurisdictions reporting were 86 percent and 90 percent, respectively.

For timeliness of purchasing services, 93 percent of customers rated service as excellent or good. The mean and median were 82 percent and 83 percent, respectively.

Reno describes its purchasing operation as decentralized, with 1.5 full-time-equivalent staff in the finance department providing support to other city departments responsible for making the purchases themselves.

The purchasing division must approve all purchase orders regardless of amount, and purchases greater than $25,000 must also receive city council approval.

Relationship building is the key

When asked how it achieves such high customer satisfaction ratings, the Reno purchasing division noted the cultivation of strong customer relationships as the key. They stated that division staff make special efforts to inform customers of

- Purchasing approval requirements
- Criteria for choosing the appropriate purchasing method (for example, bid versus request for proposal)
- General time frames for completing different types of purchases.

Purchasing staff provide this information in workshops offered throughout the year and through informal interactions during the purchasing process itself.

Accommodating unexpected demands helps, too

Reno's purchasing staff also seek to accommodate customers with unexpected purchase needs and other quick turnaround requirements quickly. It is understood that sometimes unanticipated demands arise, and helping customers meet them while adhering to guidelines of good purchasing practice is important. This also boosts customer satisfaction!

Reno raises the bar—now targeting 97 percent satisfaction

Although Reno's purchasing staff remain pleased that 93 percent of customers rate their service as excellent or good, they seek do even better; and they recently raised their goal to achieving 97 percent of ratings in the excellent and good categories. Their goal is published in the city budget.

Case Profile

Population:
206,735

Square miles:
102

Median household income:
$42,214

Form of government:
Council-manager

For additional information about the practices described in this case study, please contact Laurie Pedrick, purchasing program manager, at 775/334-2210.

City of Richmond, VA

Case Profile

Population:
193,200

Square miles:
63

Median household income:
$31,620

Form of government:
Mayor-council

Performance Indicator

- **Percentage of central purchasing office purchasing volume (in dollars) awarded to minority- and women-owned firms**

For FY 2006, the city of Richmond reported that, by dollar volume, 21 percent of all contracts awarded through the central purchasing office were awarded to minority- and women-owned firms. The mean and median values for all jurisdictions reporting were 7.8 percent and 8.3 percent, respectively.

The city further reported that 19 percent of non-construction contracts and 13 percent of construction contracts both with values greater than $100,000 and administered by the central purchasing office were awarded to minority- and women-owned firms.

Find the firms

When asked how the city achieved such good results with its minority business program, staff noted that the city of Richmond actively pursues minority-owned firms:

- Through its database of more than 900 registered minority-owned firms
- By reaching out to business leagues and minority development councils and their members.

For each project, the city's Office of Minority Business Development (OMBD) bases the goals for minority business participation on the scope of work to be performed and the availability of minority-owned firms to perform work for the project. After the participation goals are set, the city selects a vendor on the basis of experience, past performance, proposed minority participation, and other factors.

Inform the firms about relevant projects

The city's OMBD and department of procurement services then contact relevant minority-owned firms in their database. They make contact by e-mail and postal service and also post all project and bid information on the city's Web site. The OMBD also provides information about upcoming projects via its quarterly newsletter.

The OMBD surveys vendors in its database annually to determine the minority business program's relevance, obtain feedback on its effectiveness, and help identify areas of need.

Teach firms how to bid effectively

Each year after the city budget is approved, minority-owned firms are invited to attend OMBD-sponsored outreach sessions in which various departments present their capital improvement budgets and discuss the projects the city will undertake in the coming year.

Other sessions address:

- How to bid on projects successfully
- How to engage in business with the city
- The ABCs of insurance and bonding.

For additional information about the practices described in this case study, please contact Rita Henderson, director of the Office of Minority Business Development, at 804/646-5947, or Erna Robinson, director of the Department of Procurement Services, at 804/646-5796.

At the sessions, business owners are able to interact with city staff and ask questions—and prepare themselves well for the city's bidding process. The OMBD offers approximately 40 sessions that reach several hundred participants each year.

Minority-owned firms are also encouraged to schedule individual appointments with OMBD staff to discuss ways in which they can participate in city projects.

To ensure that minority-business participation goals are being met as projects progress, the OMBD requires prime contractors with proposed minority-owned business participation to report progress every month. As part of the evaluation process, the city scores firms on the basis of past minority participation performance and success in reaching minority-business participation goals.

City of University Place, WA

Case Profile

Population:
31,140

Square miles:
8

Median household income:
$54,782

Form of government:
Council-manager

Performance Indicator

- **Customer satisfaction with the timeliness of service**

For FY 2006, University Place reported that 97 percent of customers rated the timeliness of purchasing service as excellent or good. The mean and median were 82 percent and 83 percent, respectively.

Daily review of requests ensures timely processing

City staff attribute much of their success for this indicator to daily review of purchase order requests. At around 11:00 a.m. each day, the city's senior finance specialist reviews all requisitions that were submitted between the previous afternoon and that morning. Daily review of requests, as opposed to the weekly review that occurred in previous years, has increased the timeliness of approvals—and customer satisfaction—considerably.

City departments also strive to include all backup documentation required for approval of their purchase orders at the time they submit their purchase order requests, which promotes speedy approval.

Technology further speeds processing

The city of University Place also uses an off-the-shelf purchasing software package (EDEN Gold Standard, Version 4.4), which facilitates efficient processing of purchase order requests. The software allows staff to:

- Submit requisitions and supporting documentation electronically
- Check requisition status (for example, to determine who is responsible for approvals)
- Receive electronic alerts designed to inform supervisors that a requisition has been submitted in their respective departments
- Receive electronic notification when documentation is missing
- See other requisitions in the queue
- Receive electronic notification when purchase orders are completed.

Track purchasing trends to anticipate customer needs

Each month, purchasing staff review requisition data and look for patterns. Through data analysis, the city has been able to identify departmental and seasonal trends—and prepare for peaks in demand for purchasing services.

One trend found in the data is an increase in requisitions from the public works department in the spring and summer to cover road repairs, field preparations, parks maintenance, and other activities that generally require warmer weather. The data also show an increase in requisitions from the recreation department at the time of its summer festival.

Tracking these trends allows the purchasing department to anticipate customer needs and equip itself to respond and approve requisitions in a consistent and timely manner, which in turn promotes high customer satisfaction.

For additional information about the practices described in this case study, please contact Debbie Hall, senior finance specialist, at dhall@cityofup.com.

Refuse and Recycling

Refuse and Recycling

City and County of Denver, CO

Performance Indicator

- **Net operating and maintenance expenditures for recycling services per ton of recyclable material collected**

For FY 2006, the city and county of Denver reported spending a net of only $11.71 per ton for collection of recyclable material. The mean and median figures for all jurisdictions reporting on this indicator were $108.61 per ton and $97.69 per ton, respectively. (These net values reflect the jurisdictions' costs after accounting for revenue from any sales of recyclable material collected.)

Container switch saves time and reduces injuries—and saves money

In 2005, Denver switched from 18-gallon containers with manual collection to 65-gallon containers with automatic collection. The goals of the move included

- Increasing the types and quantity of recyclable material collected
- Boosting customer satisfaction by offering more convenient wheeled carts
- Reducing worker injuries by eliminating the need for staff to lift heavy recycling bins
- Improving efficiency by allowing more pickups per day per vehicle.

The city increased the number of stops per truck per eight-hour collection day by more than 60 percent, from 400 to 650.

Several major improvements resulted from the changeover:

- The city increased the number of stops per truck per eight-hour collection day by more than 60 percent, from 400 to 650.
- This in turn, allowed Denver to reduce the number of collection routes from 14 to 10.
- Customer satisfaction increased, as did the number of homeowners who chose to join the recycling program.

Another anticipated benefit of the container change is a reduction in workers' compensation premiums. Since the implementation of the automatic collection trucks, Denver has seen the number of worker injuries drop. Because premiums are based on injury rates for the prior year, Denver expects to see further cost savings for its recycling operation when premiums are recalculated in 2008.

No middleman processing boosts bottom line, too

Denver collects recyclable material from all interested residents at no direct cost to the residents themselves. Residents must request the service, and 48 percent have done so.

Case Profile

Population:
575,294

Square miles:
155

Median household income:
$42,370

Form of government:
Mayor-council

For additional information about the practices described in this case study, please contact Mike Lutz, operations manager, at 720/865-6845 or mike.lutz@denvergov.org.

The city contracts for the processing of recyclable material collected from residents. The contractor pays Denver a fixed rate of $33 per ton for 95 percent of all mixed-commodity material collected from residents (assuming that 5 percent of all material collected is not recyclable). The contract includes an "up-market" clause, stipulating that if the weighted market price for recyclable material exceeds a base value established in their contract, the contractor will share on a 50-50 annualized basis the revenue above that base value, in addition to the $33 per ton already required.

City of Johnson City, TN

Performance Indicator

- **Operating and maintenance expenditures for refuse collection per ton of refuse collected**

For FY 2006, the city of Johnson City reported operating and maintenance expenditures for refuse collection of $22.65 per ton of refuse collected. The mean and median values for all jurisdictions reporting were $53.85 per ton and $45.40 per ton, respectively.

City staff stated that a change to automated collection trucks in 2004 played a major role in helping achieve such low collection expenditures.

Johnson City provides refuse collection services to all residential and commercial customers within the city limits. This includes approximately 20,600 residential accounts and 2,600 commercial accounts. The city also owns its own landfill with operations contracted to a private company.

Johnson City notes that owning its own landfill helps the city keep disposal costs relatively low, too. The landfill is located within city limits, and the close proximity ensures that costs for travel time and fuel to transport refuse to the landfill remain as low as possible.

Support your program through reasonable fees—and other sources, if available

The city's refuse collection program is supported through user fees. Households are charged a rate of $12 per month for refuse collection services, which include

- Weekly curbside refuse (and recycling) pickup
- Twice monthly brush collection
- Seasonal leaf pickup (at least four times per year).

The city provides one refuse collection cart to each household. Households may purchase additional carts for $50 each.

The solid-waste division is an enterprise fund that operates exclusively on user fees and is not subsidized by any type of sales or property taxes. A high proportion of out-of-town visitors who eat and shop in city establishments help to boost the city's sales tax revenues above what would normally be expected for a jurisdiction the size of Johnson City. This in turn allows the city to subsidize services like refuse collection.

Use automated trucks

As noted previously, Johnson City switched from a fleet of mostly manual trucks to mostly automated collection trucks in 2004. The goals of the switch were to

- Boost route efficiency
- Promote worker safety (by minimizing injuries)
- Save money.

Case Profile

Population:
61,233

Square miles:
41

Median household income:
$30,835

Form of government:
Council-manager

For additional information about the practices described in this case study, please contact John C. Smith, solid-waste manager, at josmith@johnsoncitytn.org.

Data show that the change has worked. After moving to the automated trucks, for example, the city recorded just one workers' compensation claim between 2004 and 2008, compared with 31 claims the year before the change.

Employ other efficiency boosters

Johnson City also noted several other steps that it takes to promote refuse collection efficiency, which in turn saves money:

- **Auditing pickup data and adjusting routes as necessary**—Johnson City equips all collection trucks with counters that employees use to track the number of pickups they make each day. Managers compile these data and review the data at least semiannually to determine whether collection burdens are remaining level across routes. When the data indicate that more pickups are being required on one route than another, managers adjust the routes to even out the burden. This helps ensure that staff and trucks are being employed in the most cost-effective way possible.

The success of the city's variable merit raise system is reflected not only in the difference between the number of employees receiving adjustments in FY 2006 compared with FY 2007 but also in the fact that there has been no turnover in the city's residential refuse collection staff since 2002.

- **Offering reasonable route completion incentives**—Although many refuse collection operations promote speedy pickups by allowing workers to depart after their routes are complete, Johnson City does this with a twist. The city allows refuse collection staff to depart up to one hour early. Even if they complete their route two hours before the end of their shift, employees must continue working until one hour before the end of their shift. This system has two advantages:
  - It encourages employees to complete their routes quickly while ensuring adequate time to do the work well. (Crews even engage in informal competition to see which crew completes its route first.) The city emphasizes high-quality service provided with a positive attitude—and the incentive program reflects these values.
  - By offering employees the opportunity to depart early (within limits), the department has nearly eliminated requests for overtime—further saving money.

- **Implementing a true merit pay system**—Through FY 2005, all city employees received fixed merit pay adjustments, which made it difficult for the city to reward employees who exhibited truly exceptional performance. Thus, the city moved to system of variable merit pay increases for FY 2006. Pay rate adjustments were aligned with individual employee objectives and goals, which enabled managers to award merit raises in relation to specific employee achievements. Implementation of the new system included some growing pains, as six employees failed to achieve performance levels required to receive merit raises in FY 2006. By contrast, in FY 2007, only one employee missed the goals required to receive a merit raise. Moreover, the success of the city's variable merit raise system is reflected not only in the difference between the number of employees receiving adjustments in FY 2006 compared with FY 2007 but also in the fact that there has been no turnover in the city's residential refuse collection staff since 2002.

With all of its efficiency efforts, the city seeks to encourage safe, timely, and effective service provision along with responsible handling of city-owned machinery and citizen-owned refuse collection carts.

Don't rest on your laurels

The city looks forward to increasing refuse collection efficiency further with the implementation of geographic information system-assisted routing in 2009.

Village of Oak Park, IL

Case Profile

Population:
52,524

Square miles:
5

Median household income:
$59,183

Form of government:
Council-manager

Performance Indicator

- **Tons of recyclable material collected as a percentage of all refuse and recyclable material collected**

For FY 2006, the village of Oak Park's refuse division reported that recyclable material constituted 31.9 percent of its solid-waste stream. The mean and median proportions for all jurisdictions reporting were 13.6 percent and 10.1 percent, respectively.

Village efforts boost recycling tonnage by 24 percent

The village points to two major factors in its recycling success:

- Financial incentives to encourage residents to recycle
- Effective communication with residents about recycling opportunities.

Furthermore, the village reports that because of these efforts it boosted recycling tonnage by 24 percent and reduced refuse tonnage by 21 percent between the years 1999 and 2007.

Incentives encourage recycling (money talks!)

To encourage residents to recycle as much waste as possible, the village offers a number of incentives:

- **Free collection of recyclable material**—The village collects for free as much recyclable material as is left at the curb each week by any resident.
- **Wide variety of material accepted for recycling**—To make recycling as convenient and fruitful as possible for residents, Oak Park accepts an exceptionally wide variety of materials (for example, all plastics except type 6). The village does not require residents to sort their recyclables and assists them in disposing of tricky, hazardous items like unused paint—even facilitating swaps of reusable items between residents.
- **Container size choices allow residents to save**—Nonrecyclable material is collected for a fee, but those who choose a smaller container save money. Residents may choose from a 96-gallon container for $18.20 per month or a 64-gallon container for $15.34 per month—resulting in a savings of 16 percent for users of the smaller container. Twenty-six percent of Oak Park households take advantage of the smaller-container option.
- **Sharing containers is an option**—In some cases, residents can save even more if they choose to share a refuse container with a neighbor and split the cost.

Residents learn about options for reducing nonrecyclable waste

The village seeks to keep recycling in the forefront of residents' minds through frequent communication. Oak Park has published a general interest newsletter for the past seven years, switching in 2001 from bimonthly to monthly distribution in order to communicate more often the benefits of recycling (and other city programs).

i

For additional information about the practices described in this case study, please contact Karen Rozmus at 708/358-5707 or rozmus@oak-park.us.

Each newsletter includes at least one feature about recycling. Recent stories have addressed

- Materials that can (and can't) be recycled
- What happens to recycled materials
- Alternatives to products that come in nonrecyclable packaging.

Tracking and reporting recycling performance

The village of Oak Park tracks recycling performance quarterly, sharing the data with its nine-member Environment and Energy Citizen's Advisory Commission, residents, village board, and village manager. The village supplements this quarterly reporting with an annual review of the village's performance as compared with prior years; for this it uses data gathered by the ICMA Center for Performance Measurement™ (CPM).

City of Phoenix, AZ

Case Profile

Population:
1,507,130

Square miles:
516

Median household income:
$42,353

Form of government:
Council-manager

Performance Indicator

- **Citizen satisfaction with refuse collection services**

For FY 2006, Phoenix reported that 93 percent of customers surveyed rated the quality of refuse collection service as excellent or good. The mean and median values for all jurisdictions reporting were 86 percent and 83 percent, respectively.

The acting solid-waste administrator attributes her division's high customer service ratings to

- Phoenix's citywide culture of seamless customer service
- An in-depth customer service training program
- Managed competition for residential refuse and recycling collection.

Intensive customer service training

In 2003, Phoenix's solid-waste division conducted an intensive, year-long customer service review. Employees met approximately once each month during the year to establish customer service goals and develop plans for achieving of the goals. One output of this process was development of an intensive customer service training program for refuse collection staff. The program was developed by a professional trainer in consultation with refuse collection and other solid-waste division staff.

The training program continues today and focuses on promoting customer satisfaction by projecting a clean-cut, professional image for the city's refuse collection program. Elements of this image include

- **Sparkling clean trucks**—Refuse collection is a dirty business, and Phoenix takes great care to ensure that the city's refuse collection trucks always look clean by
  - — Washing trucks frequently
  - — Painting panels when stains appear
  - — Ensuring that tire rims match when tires are replaced
  - — Keeping dashboards clean and clear.
- **Friendly, clean-cut drivers**—Drivers wear the city's uniform shirt, and it must be clean, pressed, and free from rips, tears, or fraying. Drivers are also actively encouraged to smile and wave at customers whom they encounter on their routes. They also stock and distribute pamphlets detailing social services available through the city.
- **Careful placement of containers**—Drivers ensure that cans are always left upright at the curb after emptying. If cans tip after emptying, drivers park their trucks and return the cans to an upright position before proceeding.
- **Always going the extra mile to satisfy customers**—Drivers return to pick up missed containers any time they are asked to do so (or if they themselves notice a missed container), even if the containers were

For additional information about the practices described in this case study, please contact Cheri Ditto, acting solid-waste administrator, at cheri.ditto@phoenix.gov.

missed because the residents forgot to place them for collection by the proper time.

The city employs a fleet of fully automated side rail collection trucks, each of which is staffed by a single driver.

City staff compete with private haulers

Phoenix's refuse collection staff is also motivated to provide superior customer service by the city's managed-competition program. The city is divided into six refuse and recycling collection service areas, composed of 45,000 to 75,000 residential living units each.

City staff compete with private haulers every two years to provide service for one of the city's six service areas; the service areas are placed into competition on a rotating basis, with one area available in each biennial competition cycle. Under the terms of the program, city staff are guaranteed the privilege of providing service in an area immediately following the expiration of a contract with a private hauler. City staff must also provide service to at least 50 percent of the city at any given time.

Customer service ratings are one of several requirements considered in the award of the contract in each service area.

Currently, city staff provide service to five of the city's six service areas, serving 290,000 residential living units; a private hauler serves the one other service area, serving 75,000 residential living units.

City of Tacoma, WA

Case Profile

Population:
195,898

Square miles:
63

Median household income:
$40,290

Form of government:
Council-manager

Performance Indicator

- **Operating and maintenance expenditures for refuse collection per ton of refuse collected**

For FY 2006, the city of Tacoma reported operating and maintenance expenditures of $24.85 per ton for refuse collection. The mean and median values for all jurisdictions reporting were $53.85 per ton and $45.40 per ton, respectively.

The city of Tacoma provides all residential and most commercial refuse collection services within city limits. Collection services are provided by city staff. The city also operates its own landfill. (Tipping fees and other disposal costs are not included in the collection figures reported above.)

Tacoma's solid-waste division attributes its low refuse collection expenditures to the benefits gained from automated refuse collection.

Automation

Currently, Tacoma operates 15 fully automated residential collection routes and one semiautomated residential collection route. Yard-waste collection is fully automated, and residential recycling is currently changing from semiautomated to fully automated collection. (Yard-waste and recycling collection expenditures are not included in the operating and maintenance expenditure figures reported to the ICMA Center for Performance Measurement™ [CPM]; they are reported separately.)

With the advent of automated refuse collection, which requires fewer workers per truck than manual collection, the city proudly reports that it did not have to lay off staff. Instead, drivers no longer needed for residential refuse collection were reassigned to yard-waste, recycling, and commercial collection operations.

Teamwork

In 1998, the city of Tacoma created an area-based routing system. Under this system, the city was divided into five geographic areas (one for each day of the week), with 15 collection routes in each area.

The areas were established on the basis of population and geography to balance collection requirements across a five-day workweek. Within an area, each driver is assigned to an individual route, but all drivers work together if a particular route is unassigned on a given day.

The routing system also allows Tacoma's solid-waste division to adjust individual routes to improve collection efficiencies without affecting the customers' pickup day. This results in an efficient, flexible collection program.

City staff also noted that major growth in multifamily housing development between 2005 and 2008 may be contributing to more efficient routing and lower collection costs.

For additional information about the practices described in this case study, please contact Carol Parvey, principal engineer, at cparvey@ci.tacoma.wa.us.

City of Urbandale, IA

Performance Indicator

- **Citizen satisfaction with refuse collection services**

For FY 2006, the city of Urbandale's refuse division reported that 97.7 percent of its customers rated the quality of service as excellent or good. The mean and median values for all jurisdictions reporting were 86 percent and 83 percent, respectively.

Emphasize low-price, high-value service

When asked how they achieved such high customer satisfaction with refuse collection services, Urbandale's solid-waste staff pointed first to their "low-price, high-value" philosophy:

- Each household pays just $6 per month for refuse and recycling pickup; remaining costs are paid by general fund revenues.
- Trash and recyclable materials are picked up curbside every week.
- The city accepts a wide variety of recyclables at the curb, including non-traditional items like aerosol cans and wire hangers.
- Appointment-based pickup for logs, tree limbs, furniture, appliances, and other large items is available to all customers.
- Annual "spring cleaning" pickup of (almost) anything residents can haul to the curb is offered.

City staff are encouraged not to rest on their laurels but, rather, to seek ways to continue boosting customer satisfaction by refining existing services and introducing new lines of service. One example is a recent refinement to the city's yard-waste-collection program that has been particularly popular with customers. Previously, residents could dispose of yard waste only by using "pay-as-you-throw" bags purchased from the city. Now they have the additional option of subscribing to an annual yard-waste-collection service that offers a special bin that can be used to dispose of yard waste at the curb throughout the year without the hassle of having to purchase one-time-use bags again and again throughout the year. (The PAYT bags remain available to residents who prefer them, however.)

Boost efficiency, safety—and save $45,000 in workers' comp claims with automated trucks

Another factor that Urbandale staff cited as contributing to residents' high satisfaction was implementation of fully automated collection vehicles. The fully automated vehicles have enabled each operator to increase the number of households served per day from 500 to 900, an increase of 80 percent.

Another benefit of switching to fully automated trucks was a significant decrease in worker injuries, resulting in a decrease in workers' compensation claims and thereby significantly reducing costs for the solid-waste-collection program. During the eight years prior to the implementation of automated collection, there was an average of 2.9 incidents of injury per

Case Profile

Population:
35,904

Square miles:
22

Median household income:
$59,744

Form of government:
Council-manager

For additional information about the practices described in this case study, please contact Tim Stovie, assistant director of public works, at 515/278-3900 or tstovie@urbandale.org.

year, with an average claim cost of $45,000 per year. Since automated collection has been implemented, there have been no injury claims related to the collection of solid waste.

Promote accountability

To ensure that high customer satisfaction remains a priority in their day-to-day work, Urbandale's solid-waste-collection staff work toward an explicit goal of attaining 95 percent customer satisfaction. Performance against this goal is monitored by the city manager and published in the city's biannual citizen survey report, annual budget document, council reports, and other outlets.

During the eight years prior to the implementation of automated collection, there was an average of 2.9 incidents of injury per year, with an average claim cost of $45,000 per year. Since automated collection has been implemented, there have been no injury claims related to the collection of solid waste.

City staff track performance on this indicator over time and regularly compare Urbandale's performance with that of other communities participating the ICMA Center for Performance Measurement™ (CPM). This performance also is reflected in the annual performance evaluations of Urbandale's six solid-waste collectors. These individuals, with a combined 108 years of experience, are among the mostly highly evaluated employees in the department.

Publicize services well

In addition to putting together a comprehensive, low-cost solid-waste-collection program, the city of Urbandale also makes sure that residents know about the services available. The services are periodically described in the city's quarterly newsletter, and full descriptions of the services are available on the city's Web site. In addition, inserts in residential water bills also remind residents about value-added services like the spring cleanup and the by-appointment collection of logs and tree limbs. Last, the city takes full advantage of marketing materials provided by the Metro Waste Authority, an umbrella organization that promotes recycling in central Iowa.

Risk Management

Risk Management

City of Corpus Christi, TX

Performance Indicator

- Vehicle accident rate

In FY 2007 through its regular claims analysis program, Corpus Christi's risk management office noticed that a majority of its liability claims were related to accidents involving city vehicles. This raised particular concern for the city because of the threat to life and general safety that vehicle accidents represent. The city decided to take action to reduce the vehicle accident rate.

The city began by further reviewing the data, to be sure that its information was correct. It then modified procedures but did not see significant declines in vehicle accidents. The city then decided to examine the role of its Vehicle Accident Review Board, with the hope that further assistance from the board might help bring down the accident rate.

Board composition

The city of Corpus Christi's Vehicle Accident Review Board was established in 1996. It comprises 15 members who meet monthly to review all vehicle accidents that occurred in the prior month; the purpose of the reviews is to determine whether the accidents were preventable. Board members are appointed by the city manager and include employees from various city departments, including the solid waste, police, fire, streets, and parks departments.

The risk management department also works directly to help ensure vehicle accident accountability. Each quarter, the risk management department produces a report that analyzes (among other indicators) the vehicle accident rate citywide.

To ensure that board members are able to accurately assess vehicle accidents, they receive annual training that includes policy and procedure review and case study analysis.

Accident review

For each accident, board members begin by conducting a review of all documents related to the accident:

- Police reports
- Employee statements
- Any other related material.

Employees and other people who may have been involved in the accident do not appear before the board as a part of this review.

Following the document review, board members discuss the accident and apply a numerical rating to the accident, which represents the accident's seriousness and preventability. Employees then receive written notification of the board's decision and may appeal if they desire.

Case Profile

Population:
294,160

Square miles:
504

Median household income:
$39,698

Form of government:
Mayor-council

For additional information about the practices described in this case study, please contact Donna James-Spruce, risk manager, at donnaj@cctexas.com.

The appeal is a separate process that includes the board's chair and vice chair, the city's risk manager, and a representative of the employee's department. The employee's supervisor usually also attends the appeal. Unlike the first review, the employee attends the appeal and has the opportunity to discuss the accident in person with members of the Appeals Board. The employee may also ask the Appeals Board about its decision.

All levels of management involved

To ensure accountability in all areas of city operations, the city of Corpus Christi uses balanced scorecards. At the city manager's request, vehicle accident rate is one of the scorecard indicators for every department that uses city vehicles.

The city manager meets with department heads monthly to discuss their scorecards, and department heads may review each other's scorecards, including each other's vehicle accident rates.

The risk management department also works directly to help ensure vehicle accident accountability. Each quarter, the risk management department produces a report that analyzes (among other indicators) the vehicle accident rate citywide. The department also compiles an annual report of risk management indicators that is circulated among staff and presented to the city council.

Since modifying the role of the Vehicle Accident Review Board and instituting multifaceted performance measurement reporting, the city of Corpus Christi has achieved a substantial decrease in vehicle accidents. For the first six months of fiscal year 2008, the number of total preventable motor vehicle accidents decreased 49 percent from the same period the prior year.

City of Mesa, AZ

Performance Indicator

- **Total property loss, premiums, and other expenditures per $1,000 of property value at risk**

For FY 2006, the city of Mesa reported total property loss, premiums, and other expenditures of $1.04 per $1,000 of property value at risk. The mean and median values for all other jurisdictions reporting were $3.86 and $2.21, respectively.

In addition to a somewhat soft insurance market and favorable climate, which currently benefit many Sunbelt communities, the city of Mesa attributes much of its success in keeping risk management costs low to its well-researched insurance program and staff education program.

City's self-insurance program features $50,000 deductible, chargeable to the claiming department

The city's self-insurance program features a $50,000 deductible. Moreover, when a claim is filed, this deductible is ultimately paid by the division responsible for the claim; the city does not centrally fund insurance deductibles. Most losses are valued at less than $50,000, and the cost of such losses is absorbed by the responsible department. Thus, departments have a vested interest in minimizing claims in order to preserve their funds.

Research on commercial policies saved $103,000

The city also carefully researches the commercial policies it buys. For example, in 2006, rather than simply renewing the city's existing property policy, risk management staff contacted neighboring local governments and canvassed insurance providers, finding that market prices had dropped. Based on their research, they chose to procure coverage from a new provider, reducing their annual costs by $103,000 (from $360,000 to $257,000). Had they not conducted their research, they would not have had the negotiating power to reduce expenditures so greatly.

City educates employees about worker safety and the costs of accidents

The risk management division assists departments in their efforts to minimize insurance claims by educating employees about safe working practices and the financial implications of unsafe activities. Furthermore, the content and frequency of the education programs are based on the work activities and risk profile of each department.

Most education sessions feature information about

- Safe driving
- Safe tool use
- Replacement value of vehicles and tools
- Deductible costs, and the fact that the responsible division pays.

Case Profile

Population:
455,984

Square miles:
131

Median household income:
$44,861

Form of government:
Council-manager

For additional information about the practices described in this case study, please contact Barry Hegrenes, risk manager, at barry.hegrenes@cityofmesa.org.

The city's risk management division also maintains a ready access policy regarding claim records, meaning that departments in the city may request their claim records at any time. This relates directly to the risk management division's emphasis on education; the division seeks to provide as much information as possible to promote departments' understanding of claim costs—all with the goal of reducing future claims.

City monitors risk management expenditures

Claim amounts and other risk management expenditures are closely monitored by the risk management division and the city attorney's office. They are also tracked indirectly through the city's financial reporting system and balanced scorecard program. (Legal requirements prevent disclosure of some claim details in the public reporting processes.)

City of Salem, OR

Performance Indicator

- **Total property loss, premiums, and other expenditures per $1,000 of property value at risk**

For FY 2006, the city of Salem reported spending just $0.83 in risk management expenditures per $1,000 of property value at risk. For all jurisdictions reporting that year, the mean was $3.86, and the median was $2.21.

City works closely with insurance broker and carrier

To keep premiums as low as possible, the city works closely with its broker to ensure that the broker has the fullest picture possible of the city's insurance needs and its efforts to minimize property loss, which helps the broker find the carrier offering the most reasonable policy possible in terms of both cost and coverage. The city also remains in contact with its property insurance carrier throughout the year to ensure that risk associated with any new properties is managed properly.

City's strict codes minimize risk—and expenditures—for city

To promote the health and safety of residential- and commercial-building occupants throughout the city, the city has developed over the years a set of very stringent building and fire codes. One direct, although perhaps unintended, benefit of these codes has been lower-than-average risk management expenditures for the city government itself.

By conforming to its own stringent building regulations when constructing new city government facilities and enforcing the fire code strictly on its existing facilities, the city of Salem has been able to keep property losses small and garner competitive property insurance rates.

The city also enjoys favorable weather conditions, which helps minimize risk associated with hurricanes, tornadoes, and other weather-related events that may contribute to higher loss and premium expenditures in other places.

Case Profile

Population:
147,250

Square miles:
47

Median household income:
$54,200

Form of government:
Council-manager

For additional information about the practices described in this case study please contact: Sharee Emmons, risk manager, at 503/588-6132 or semmons@cityofsalem.net

Tualatin Hills Park and Recreation District, OR

Case Profile

Population:
212,985

Square miles:
60

Median household income:
Not available

Form of government:
Council-manager

Performance Indicator

- **Light vehicle traffic accidents per 100,000 miles driven**

For FY 2006, the Tualatin Hills Park and Recreation District reported 0.37 light vehicle traffic accidents per 100,000 miles driven. The mean and median values for all jurisdictions reporting were 0.69 and 0.37. Although Tualatin Hills performed at the median for this indicator in FY 2006, the district is considered an example of particularly strong performance because it was able to reduce its accident rate significantly from 2.21 accidents per 100,000 miles the previous year.

When asked how Tualatin Hills had been able to achieve this reduction in its accident rate, district personnel cited the following factors:

- **Accident analysis and follow-up training**—When examining the accidents from the previous year, district staff noticed that most of the accidents had occurred with less experienced, part-time drivers attempting difficult maneuvers like braking with trailers in tow and backing up larger vehicles. To remedy this, the district instituted additional driver training for these employees, focusing on the tricky situations in which most of the accidents had occurred.
- **Driver acceptability matrix**—The district also created a table of information that helps determine employees' driving privileges on the basis of their driving records (including accident history and moving violations). When drivers reach certain thresholds, their district driving privileges may be suspended.
- **Direct link to Oregon Department of Motor Vehicles**—To ensure that its driver acceptability matrix can be used to maximum advantage, the district has subscribed to a program offered by the Oregon DMV that generates a communication to the district within one week of an infraction by one of its employee drivers—meaning that information about any accidents or moving violations involving district drivers is delivered and can be addressed in real time. Previously, the district received driving record information through an annual review of the database of an external background check company.

For additional information about the practices described in this case study, please contact Ann E. Mackiernan, operations analyst, at 503/614-1215 or amackiernan@thprd.org.

Youth Services

Youth Services

County of Napa, CA

Performance Indicator

- **Percentage of children and youth who successfully completed conditions of their probation during the reporting period**

For FY 2006, the county of Napa reported that 85 percent of children and youth successfully completed the conditions of their probation. The mean and median values for all jurisdictions reporting were 75 percent and 79 percent, respectively.

Sentence accordingly

Napa County courts consider successful probation terms to be those for which youth can complete all of their court orders for treatment, community service, and restitution.

The supervising probation officer works with the youth and the youth's family through office, home, and school visits to assure all court orders are followed. The probation officer may also employ curfews, drug testing, and restrictions on the youth's associations with troubled friends to boost the likelihood of the youth completing probation successfully.

Although the term completion rate does not capture the duration of each youth's probation, courts usually align the end of a youth's probation term with the youth's 18th birthday; in exceptional circumstances, probationary terms may be extended beyond that date.

Intervene early

In addition to ensuring that youth assigned to probation complete their terms successfully, Napa County also applies significant resources to keeping at-risk youth from entering the probation program—or other parts of the juvenile justice system.

In about 300–400 cases each year, youth who have committed a low-risk crime such as petty theft, or have been involved in fights at school, or have shown others signs of being at-risk are assigned a social worker who assesses what is needed to divert the youth from the criminal justice system—in other words, to prevent the youth from entering the probation program. This may include meeting with a social worker or police staff, receiving counseling, or performing community service.

Such early intervention helps turn around problem behavior for many youth and may prevent them from entering the juvenile justice system altogether. The program has not completed a full evaluation to determine the exact number of youth diverted from the juvenile justice system, but early anecdotal evidence is promising.

Case Profile

Population:
132,339

Square miles:
754

Median household income:
$51,912

Form of government:
Council-administrator/manager

For additional information about the practices described in this case study, please contact Mary Butler, chief probation officer, at mbutler@co.napa.ca.us.

City of Scottsdale, AZ

Case Profile

Population:
226,390

Square miles:
185

Median household income:
$65,361

Form of government:
Council-manager

Performance Indicator

- **Percentage of children and youth ordered to perform community service who completed 100 percent of hours ordered**

For FY 2006, the city of Scottsdale's youth services division reported that 94 percent of children and youth completed 100 percent of the community service hours ordered. The mean and median values for all jurisdictions reporting were 83 percent and 86 percent, respectively.

Active engagement, it's key

When asked how the city achieved such high performance with regard to community service hours completed, a representative from Scottsdale's Youth and Family Services Program cited two important factors:

1. High level of engagement with assigned youth and their parents (or guardians)
2. Programs and service sites that are interesting to assigned youth.

Professional counselors foster an understanding of consequence

Scottsdale seeks to provide youth assigned to community service with a comprehensive intervention experience that will ensure their success in the program—and prevent them from reoffending. One aspect of this comprehensive approach is the requirement that all youth engage in a diversion intake session with a professional counselor. Parents (or guardians) must also participate in the diversion intake session.

Through the diversion program, community service program staff seek to provide assigned youth with a more mature perspective on the actions that brought them to the program and encourage them to make better choices in the future. It is important to note, too, that counselors may address problems outside the scope of the event that brought the child to the community service program. As noted previously, the approach is intended to be comprehensive, and it is aimed at preventing future problems as well as addressing current ones.

Another noted feature of the diversion program is the exit interview, during which counselors trace with assigned youth the course of events from the incident that precipitated their assignment to the program through the completion of their sentence. The goal is to help participating youth make the connection between their actions and the corresponding consequences.

In addition to the sessions with the counselors, assigned youth are also required to attend workshops that promote better decision making with regard to friendships, drugs and alcohol, and other relevant topics. A number of workshops are offered throughout the year, and youth are allowed to choose the topics that interest them most.

This intensive engagement through the diversion and workshop components of Scottsdale's community service program plays a major role in

i

For additional information about the practices described in this case study, please contact Hugh McGill, manager of youth and family services, at hmcgill@scottsdaleaz.gov.

ensuring that nearly all assigned youth complete the full terms of their community service obligations.

Parks and recreation support further promotes sentence completion

Another factor that helps keep youth engaged so successfully with the city's community service program is the participation of the city's parks and recreation department. Most community service hours are served at city parks and recreation sites under supervision of parks and recreation staff.

Some of the program's best results have been achieved at one of the city's fitness centers, where assigned youth are responsible for cleaning the workout machines. While completing these assignments, the youth frequently interact with the sport and fitness trainers who work there—and mentoring relationships have developed between the youth and the trainers in a number of cases. A benefit of this mentoring has been that some youth have begun spending more free time at the fitness center instead of in other more risky environments, further encouraging them to complete their community service and decreasing their likelihood of reoffending.

County of Washoe, NV

Case Profile

Population:
396,844

Square miles:
6,600

Median household income:
$48,865

Form of government:
Council-administrator/manager

Performance Indicator

- **Percentage of children and youth ordered to perform community service who completed 100 percent of hours ordered**

In FY 2006, Washoe County reported that 90 percent of youth assigned to its community service program completed all hours assigned. For all jurisdictions reporting, the mean and median completion rates were 83 percent and 86 percent, respectively.

Washoe County attributes its success in having youth assigned to its community service program complete their hours to its well-trained and supportive staff and its safe, engaging program of activities.

Formal and informal referrals

In Washoe County, youth may be referred to the community service program through formal or informal means. Formal referrals come from the juvenile and traffic courts as part of a sentence. Informal referrals may be made by parents or social workers concerned about risky behavior on the part of children in their care.

Once they enter the program, community service participants are engaged by contract to complete their obligation and to allow staff to monitor their progress. Participants receive rewards and consequences based on their progress.

Train and support staff

Youth referred for community service perform their work in 14-member groups that are directly supervised by a work program field supervisor, who is an adult employee of the probation department specially trained to work with at-risk youth. Field supervisors may be part-time or full-time employees.

- **Full-time staff interact with youth in multiple capacities**—Because the program operates only when the children are out of school, supervisors in full-time positions usually perform other work, like teaching behavioral competency classes and supervising other youth during the week. This provides opportunities for such staff to reinforce relationships with and provide more intensive support to youth who may be enrolled in multiple probation department programs. Part-time positions are frequently filled by local college students studying social work, psychology, or other related subjects—and who demonstrate a sincere interest in working with at-risk youth.
- **New staff receive extensive training and support**—All new supervisors spend 32–40 hours shadowing an experienced supervisor before supervising their own groups. When they begin supervising their own groups, new supervisors and their groups work side by side for 8–12 crew days with an experienced supervisor and the veteran supervisor's group to provide the new supervisor with on-the-spot support for challenging situations and to monitor the performance of new supervisor. All supervisors also complete an after action report each day.

For additional information about the practices described in this case study, please contact Carey Stewart, division director, early intervention, Juvenile Services Department, at cstewart@washoecounty.us.

- **In training, supervisors are taught techniques for building rapport with reluctant kids**—The supervisors are shown how to assign tasks based on children's capacity with regard to physical strength and other attributes. They also receive training in driver safety and cardio-pulmonary resuscitation.

Offer safe, engaging projects

Community service projects performed by youth in the Washoe County program include:

- Building hiking and biking trails in county parks
- Removing litter and natural debris from county parks
- Removing litter from other sites.

Safety of the children performing community service is a major concern of program administrators. Because of this, program participants are not permitted to remove litter from roadways or other unprotected areas; if working near a roadway, the young people must perform all activities behind safety barriers.

Provide youth with rewards and consequences

As described earlier, upon entering Washoe County's community service program, participating youth must sign a contract committing to complete their assigned hours. For those who are formally referred by the courts, consequences apply if they are late arriving, if they malinger during work time, and if they fail to complete their hours. The usual consequence is additional community service time. If a child arrives late to a work session, for example, a one-day extension of the community service obligation can be applied.

Officially referred children who are absent from three or more work sessions without a valid excuse are referred back to their probation officer who returns them to court for reconsideration of the most appropriate sentence for the offense that sent them to the community service program. They may also be referred to detention for an hour-for-hour makeup of the hours skipped in the community service program. Hours in this makeup detention are not reported in statistics of successful completion for the community service program; they simply satisfy the child's sentencing obligation.

Youth who perform well by arriving on time, behaving courteously toward staff and fellow group members, and working to the best of their ability can reduce the time required to fulfill their community service obligations by up to one day for every three days that they have been assigned.

All children also participate in an end-of-day review; at that time they have the opportunity to discuss what went well during their community service that day and what they might do better the next day.

Conclusion

By training staff well, selecting safe activities, and engaging youth with careful application of rewards and consequences, Washoe County has constructed a youth community service program that encourages completion of assigned hours.

WASHOE COUNTY DEPARTMENT OF JUVENILE SERVICES WORK PROGRAM

FILL IN ALL SHADED AREA, IF APPLICABLE - PRINT FIRMLY

MINOR ______ LAST FIRST MIDDLE INITIAL | DAYS ASSN

P.O. ______

DATES ASSN ___/___/___/___/___ PRIORS

HOME PHONE: ______ WORK PHONE: ______

COURT COMMENTS (Offense, etc.)

SPECIFIC OFFENSE:

PARENT'S NAME:

DATE OF OFFENSE:

ADDRESS:

SPECIAL INSTRUCTIONS: See Medical

UNIT	INFORMAL	COURT ORDERED	SEX	AGE	D.O.B.

MEDICAL

LIST KNOWN MEDICAL PROBLEMS, REACTIONS TO MEDICATIONS, SEVERE ALLERGIES, ETC.

I. WAIVER OF PHYSICAL EXAMINATION
This is to certify that to the best of my knowledge, my child is physically capable of participating in work projects involving physical labor. I hereby give my consent for his/her participation in this program without a physical examination.

II. AUTHORIZATION FOR MEDICAL TREATMENT
I hereby authorize and give my consent to medical, surgical, and dental diagnostic procedures or treatment including, but not limited to, physical examination, inoculations, and therapeutic treatment of my child whenever any of the foregoing is deemed necessary by a licensed physician or dentist.

PROGRAM RULES

Your work habits, attitude, and willingness to participate in this program will be evaluated by your Field Supervisor. This evaluation will be made available to the Court.

I. ATTENDANCE/ABSENTEEISM

1. The hours of every workday are 7:30 a.m. to 3:30 p.m.
2. You must report to 650 Ferrari-McLeod at the designated time – RAIN OR SHINE. If you are late, your grade will be reduced, or you may be sent home and given an unexcused absence.
3. The only acceptable excuse for not reporting for work will be due to a death in the family. All absences due to illness must be verified by a doctor's excuse – no exceptions.
4. Transportation to 650 Ferrari-McLeod is a **PARENTAL RESPONSIBILITY.** No excuse concerning lack of transportation or auto failure will normally be accepted.
5. Any unexcused absence or unsatisfactory day will result in a penalty day, and may mean your suspension from the work program, and return to Juvenile Court.
6. In case of absence or emergency, it is **YOUR** responsibility to contact this office at **325-7919 PRIOR** to 7:30 a.m. on the scheduled workday.

II. BEHAVIOR/DRESS

1. You must remain with, and follow the instructions of your assigned supervisor, and rules of the program throughout the workday. You must not leave the work site or the field of vision of your supervisor without permission.
2. Keep busy. It should not be necessary to be reminded to do your job. Break-time will be provided by your supervisor. Make sure you understand what your supervisor wants and how they want it done.
3. Any disruptive behavior, failure to comply with program rules, abuse of tools or equipment, including vehicles or other non-compliances will result in suspension and return to Juvenile Court or penalty days. Conversely, if you receive an excellent score on two (2) consecutive days without an unexcused absence, one day will be removed from the last day of your assignment.
4. While on the work program there will be **NO SMOKING.** Items such as tobacco, matches, lighters, drugs, knives, etc., are not to be possessed. If illegal contraband or weapons are suspected, you will be subject to search and arrest. Unnecessary money, valuables, backpacks, and purses should be left at home.
5. You must wear shoes and clothes which provide comfort and **safety.** Boots are preferred – sandals, shorts, and tank tops are not acceptable. Work gloves are strongly recommended and **LONG PANTS** are mandatory.
6. Clothes that could be considered gang related such as colored bandanas, belts or shoelaces; initialed belt buckles, or shirt or pants with calligraphy or graffiti are prohibited and may result in being sent home and a penalty day.
7. Hard hat and colored vest will be provided, and without exception, will be worn at all times. These are the only clothing items that will be furnished.
8. Some worksites may be located along local highways with work zones provided by the State of Nevada Department of Transportation. These sites can experience heavy traffic at times. Participants are instructed to maintain a safe distance from the roadways at all times.
9. Work will mainly consist of litter removal and landscaping, using standard tools such as rakes or shovels. Work will not consist of any heavy lifting or use of power tools. All persons are covered under Workman's Compensation.
10. While on the worksite, participants are instructed to inform their supervisor if they encounter any hazardous materials such as animal carcasses, sharp objects, hypodermic needles, glass, razor blades or weapons. These items will be removed by staff only and must not be touched by participants.
11. As parents, it is your responsibility to see that your child arrives promptly **WITH A BAG LUNCH** at the assigned meeting location.
12. The program rules will be explained in detail prior to each workday.

INFORMAL CONTRACTUAL AGREEMENT

Minor and parent(s) are aware that they do not have to agree to proposed work program participation. They may request that the matter be heard at a formal court proceeding. By agreeing to participate on the work program, minor admits that the charged offense is true. Minor and parent(s) agree that participating on the work program is a reasonable disposition and that failure to abide by this agreement will result in the filing of a petition with the Juvenile Court and possible confinement of the minor and additional expense to the parents. Minor and parent(s) agree to waive physical examination, authorize emergency treatment and abide by the program rules.

Minor's Signature ______ Probation Officer ______

Parent or Guardian Signature ______ Date ______

Work contract for the Washoe County Department of Juvenile Services.

ICMA Center for Performance Measurement Information/Enrollment Form

☐ **Yes, my jurisdiction would like to participate in the following ICMA comparative performance measurement program[1]:**

☐ **CPM Comprehensive Program**
$5,550 annual fee (plus $4,000 one-time fee for two days of on-site training)

☐ **CPM-SC (small communities)**
$2,675 annual fee* (remote training included)
* I understand that this option is for communities with a population of 10,000 or less.

☐ **CPM-ALC (à la carte)**
$1,625 annual fee (1 service area; remote training incl.)
$2,675 annual fee (2 service areas; remote training incl.)

For CPM-ALC, please indicate the one or two service area(s) in which your jurisdiction will participate.

☐ Code Enforcement
☐ Fire & EMS
☐ Highway & Road
☐ Maintenance
☐ Information Technology
☐ Parks & Recreation
☐ Purchasing
☐ Risk Management
☐ Facilities Management
☐ Fleet Management
☐ Housing
☐ Human Resources
☐ Library Services
☐ Police
☐ Refuse & Recycling
☐ Youth Services

Workshops & other services

☐ The Essentials of Performance Measurement (full-day workshop for local government employees; $4,000)

☐ "Leadership, Management, and the Role of Performance Measurement" (half-day workshop designed for city and county managers, department heads, and team leaders and supervisors; $3,300)

☐ Legislating for Results: Performance Measurement for Elected Officials (half-day workshop for council members, county supervisors, and other elected officials; $3,300). *Note: Multiple cities and counties can split the fee if they agree to be trained* together.

☐ National Citizen Survey™ ($9,600 for the standard service)

☐ Technical assistance, peer-to-peer assistance, customized services and training (call for details).

[1] Listed fees will increase on January 1, 2009.

Name

Title

Jurisdiction

FY close (month) Population

Address

City/State/Zip

Phone Fax

E-mail

❑ **No, my jurisdiction is not ready to enroll. But I would like an ICMA representative to contact me to discuss the performance measurement program.**

Please mail or fax this form to:

ICMA Center for Performance Measurement
777 North Capitol St., N.E., Suite 500
Washington, DC 20002-4201
Fax: 202/962-3603

For vendor purposes: ICMA's Federal ID number is: 362-16-7755.

You may also contact CPM by

E-mail: cpmmail@icma.org
Phone: 202/962-3562
icma.org/performance

Publications

- *Comparative Performance Measurement: Annual Data Report* ($80 local governments; $395 private sector)
- *Does Your Government Measure Up? Basic Tools for Local Officials and Citizens* ($20)
- *Fleet Management IQ Report* ($16.95)
- *Performance Measures and Benchmarks in Local Government Facilities Maintenance* ($40)
- *Citizen Surveys: How to Do Them, How to Use Them, What They Mean*, second edition ($45)

Please visit the ICMA online bookstore **(bookstore.icma.org)** to order publications.